Television and the Gulf War

For Jim and Dorothy Gendle

Television and the Gulf War

David E. Morrison

Institute of Communications Studies
University of Leeds, UK

Acamedia Research Monograph 7

John Libbey

LONDON · PARIS · ROME

British Library Cataloguing in Publication Data

Morrisson, David E.
    Television and the Gulf War

    I. Title

ISSN: 0956-9057
ISBN: 0 86196 341 5

Series editor: Manuel Alvarado

Published by

John Libbey & Company Ltd, 13 Smiths Yard, Summerley Street,
London SW18 4HR, England
Telephone: 081-947 2777 – Fax: 081-947 2664
John Libbey Eurotext Ltd, 6 rue Blanche, 92120 Montrouge, France
John Libbey - C.I.C. s.r.l., via Lazzaro Spallanzani 11, 00161 Rome, Italy

Contents

Acknowledgements

This study was financially supported from a variety of sources. The survey and the adult group discussions were made possible by a grant from the British Broadcasting Corporation, the Independent Television Commission and the Broadcasting Standards Council. Extra funds for the children's group discussions were provided by the ITC. The overall framework which made the research possible was due to a generous donation in 1975 to the University of Leeds, which created the West Yorkshire Media in Politics Group.

The conducting of the content analysis was made possible by a grant from the Economic and Social Research Council.

Empirical research is expensive. The Institute of Communications Studies is therefore extremely grateful to the above bodies for supporting the research. Without their assistance it could not have been undertaken.

I should like to thank in particular Robin MacGregor of the BBC's Broadcasting Research Department for his constant encouragement, and Dr Barrie Gunter, Head of Research at the ITC for his enthusiasm for the project, and for his wisdom in suggesting that conducting group discussions with children was essential. I should also like to thank Colin Shaw, Director of the BSC, for financially supporting the work, but more importantly for his friendliness towards myself, and his encouragement to research. Andrea Millwood Hargrave, Research Director of the BSC, also deserves my special thanks for her enthusiasm for the project.

Michael Svennevig, Director at Research International and Head of its Media Division, cannot be thanked enough. His contribution to the study went far beyond what one might expect of the most professional market research company in terms of knowledge, time and understanding of the problems of conducting social research in the area of television. Thanks must also go to his colleague, Jo McIlvenna, whose ability to operationalize complex areas of questioning was truly instructive. The presence of Julian Bond, deputy Managing Director of Research International, was felt throughout.

Special thanks ought to be given to Dr Guy Cumberbatch and Andrea Maguire and the rest of the Communications Research Group at Aston University for their toil in coding and analysing the content analysis, and for their continuing exertions as the content analysis goes on. Thanks must also go to Dr Alison Lyon, of the research company Counterpoint, for her assistance with the children's group discussions.

The ESRC deserves special acknowledgement. A research grant provided funds, not only for the content analysis part of the research – of which the findings presented here are simply the first and small part of the full analysis that awaits completion, but also for work on experimental editing of news and interview work with journalists and editors that is to follow.

As always it is one's close colleagues that assist on a day-to-day basis whose help is particularly appreciated, but who often get taken for granted. I could never take Nicholas Pronay for granted. It was Nicholas, as Head of the Department, who originally considered that the Institute ought to study television's coverage of the Gulf. It was also Nicholas's foresight in equipping the Institute with superb satellite receiving facilities, that made possible the recording of the news from so many channels. Dr Philip Taylor, whose own book on the propaganda aspect of the war *War and the Media: Propaganda and Persuasion in the Gulf War*, Manchester University Press, is due out shortly, has been a most loyal comrade in arms, providing both ideas and general intellectual excitement to the project.

I should like also to thank Dr Brent MacGregor for his thoughtful comments on the images of news. Andy Thorpe was the technician in charge of organizing the recording of the massive amount of footage generated by the Gulf War from around the world. It is to his professional credit that we only lost one night's European recording due to snow on the satellite dishes, for which he cannot be held responsible. Christine Bailey must be mentioned in dispatches for her patient overseeing of the completion of the manuscript.

The publisher John Libbey is to be congratulated for such rapid publication of this book in their Acamedia series.

The findings presented in this book are part of a vast amount of data that has been collected and continues to be collected on the coverage of the Gulf War and the audience's response to viewing the war. The Institute of Communications Studies will be producing further volumes on a whole variety of aspects of the coverage of the war.

Introduction

In the last eight years Britain has twice sent its forces to fight abroad, first in the South Atlantic, and most recently in the Gulf. In both cases its forces have returned wearing the laurels of victory. However, whereas the performance of the British troops has never been questioned, the performance of British television has. Indeed, the 'fog of war', as military forces clash, has its media counterpart in the 'confusion of senses' about what the role of television ought to be in covering such conflict.

The research reported here set out to explore what the viewer considered the role of television ought to be in covering war and to provide an account of how viewers responded to the images they did see and the information they received.

To achieve this, the research:

(a) surveyed a representative sample of 1015 adults within Britain, and an additional 111 adults who were connected to cable television. The survey was conducted in-home and took 55 minutes for viewers to complete (Appendix 1).

(b) surveyed a sample of 212 children of parents in the main sample and conducted four group discussions with children (Appendix 2).

(c) conducted 10 adult group discussions split for age, class and sex in the North of England, the Midlands and the South of England (Appendix 3). The adult groups were shown news clips of the Amiriya bunker/shelter bombing from ITN, BBC and the French Channel TF1. In addition, raw footage was shown from the news agency WTN, that had not been broadcast because ITN considered it too harrowing.

1

(d) conducted group discussions with four sets of children living in the North and South of England.

(e) conducted a massive content analysis of the main evening news and current affairs programmes broadcast during the war on BBC1, BBC2, ITV, Channel 4, CNN and BSkyB. In addition, the news on the following foreign channels was also recorded for the purpose of comparative content analysis – Germany (BR2), France (TF1), Italy (RAI 1) and Russia (the main service carried on the Gorizont satellite).

Much of the content analysis is still to be completed, and the findings presented here are preliminary results.

The audience part of the research was funded by monies provided on a consortium basis from the BBC, BSC, ITC and the University of Leeds. The content analysis, which is on-going, was funded by a grant from the Economic and Social Research Council.

1. The Audience

MEDIA JUDGEMENT

In examining how viewers judge the performance of news there is a danger of becoming too television-centred and forgetting that as a source of information it is but one medium amongst others. It is also easy to overlook the fact that when the news on television is criticized, it does not necessarily follow that such criticism revolves on the central tenets of performance such as accuracy, bias or depth of coverage of an issue. People wish to be entertained or, if not entertained, at least not bored. Not everyone, in other words, addresses the news from the perspective of the serious student of politics or world affairs. Indeed, if that were not the case, it would be difficult to account for newspaper readership in Britain. *The Sun*, for example, has the highest circulation of any newspaper in Britain, but when we asked what newspapers the viewers read most frequently and then asked for their main reason for reading that paper, the main reason given by *Sun* readers for their selection was 'amusing/entertaining' (23 per cent), followed by 'good sports coverage' (21 per cent). The next most frequent reason given for reading the *Sun*, was 'good British news' (14 per cent). 'Good foreign news' was less likely to be nominated as a main reason for buying the paper than the fact that it carries 'bingo/prize draws/games'. This is perhaps just as well, since when readers were asked how accurate/reliable they considered their paper to be in covering world events, 4 per cent of *Sun* readers considered it not at all accurate, 33 per cent not very accurate, 51 per cent fairly accurate and 8 per cent very accurate. If we compare *Sun* readers' estimations of their paper with those of *Mirror* readers' estimations of their paper, the picture of trust is very different – 2 per cent of *Mirror* readers considered it not at all accurate, 10 per cent not very accurate, 58 per cent fairly accurate and 22 per cent very accurate. The picture of trust is pretty much the same in the area of reporting social issues

3

and political news, but trust does rise amongst readers of the *Sun* for its reportage of human interest stories – 9 per cent considered it not at all accurate, 27 per cent not very accurate, 36 per cent fairly accurate and 20 per cent considered it very accurate.

It is quite clear, then – and the *Sun* is used as an example rather than a case in point – that *Sun* readers have a different set of expectations for their paper than, say, readers of the *Mirror*, and it is these expectations that determine the judgement of performance: if *Sun* readers were not happy with their paper, then the popular would hardly be popular. The act of purchase is a very good indicator of acceptance.

The point to stress is that in judging the performance of any media we need to know two basic things, namely the values which people hold towards issues that are being reported, and the expectations which they have of performance.

We will look first (but only briefly since will we return to this theme later in examining attitudes to censorship) at the expectations of performance of television and then look, in some detail, at the values which people held towards the war.

EXPECTATIONS OF PERFORMANCE

For the great majority of people, television was their principal source of news about the Gulf War: 76 per cent said that television had provided the best coverage, compared with 10 per cent naming radio, and only 7 per cent opting for the press. This was the case across all age, sex, social grade and political groups.

Everyone interviewed was also asked to give their views on media coverage of the Gulf in terms of their satisfaction with television, radio and press coverage. Most (86 per cent) were satisfied with television coverage, their most-listened to radio service (75 per cent of all who regularly listened to radio), or their regular newspaper (84 per cent of those reading a paper regularly). The seemingly lower level of satisfaction with radio stems from the high level of 'don't know' responses – 18 per cent of listeners, compared with 2 per cent for television, and 7 per cent for newspapers. As far as newspapers were concerned, few readers said they were not satisfied with the coverage offered by their regular paper, although readers of the *Sun* were the most likely to say they were not satisfied (16 per cent of those reading it regularly), compared with the average of 5 per cent for all readers.

4

But as we have seen, readers of the *Sun* do not buy the paper primarily for news; nor do they particularly trust it to report world events with much accuracy. It is therefore reasonable to presume that lower expectations mute criticism. Even so, it could not escape scoring the highest level of dissatisfaction with its coverage compared to other papers and to other media. Given that the *Sun* is the highest circulation newspaper, it is perhaps just as well that television exists to counter – despite the *Sun*'s attacks on what it often sees as biased television reporting – the poor news information service with which the paper provides its readers.

Expectations of performance are, by and large, probably determined by actual performance; that is, by what viewers have come to expect through judging a channel on routine daily performance. When asked, early on in the questionnaire, 'how accurate/reliable do you consider the news reporting to be' on the four main channels, plus CNN and Sky, it was obvious that a great deal of trust existed towards television news on the part of the viewer.

What is obvious from Table 1 is that all the channels performed well in terms of the viewers' willingness to trust the news, especially BBC1 with 36 per cent considering its news to be very accurate.

Table 1
"How accurate/reliable do you consider the news reporting of the following to be?"

	BBC1	BBC2	ITV	C4	Sky News	CNN
Sample base	1015	1015	1015	1015	1015	1015
Weighted base	1015	1015	1015	1015	1015	1015
Very	363	275	286	216	47	24
	36%	27%	28%	21%	5%	2%
Fairly	550	447	621	396	53	33
	54%	44%	61%	39%	5%	3%
Not very	34	40	48	36	7	10
	3%	4%	5%	4%	1%	1%
Not at all	1	1	3	10	5	2
	*	*	*	1%	*	*
Don't know/not stated	67	252	56	357	903	946
	7%	25%	6%	35%	89%	93%

Base: All respondents.

Table 2. Reasons for dissatisfaction with media coverage

	Newspaper Readers %	Radio Listeners %	Television Viewers %
Not informative enough	15	18	8
Repetitive	14	11	43
Not always trustworthy	11	3	6
Too much space devoted to the war	10	10	38
Not very balanced	10	2	7
Not accurate	6	2	6
Did not always keep to the facts	6	2	5
Not up-to-date	6	1	3
Boring	4	2	5
Too little coverage	1	7	–
Too much speculation	1	–	6
Disrupted normal programmes	–	4	12
Other replies including 'Don't know'	34	54	29
Unweighted base:	460	469	507

Base: All not very satisfied with each medium's coverage.
Note: 'Other' replies are all those given by under 5 per cent in all three groups. Replies were given verbatim, and coded into the categories shown above during the interview. Total replies can exceed 100 per cent per medium, as more than one reason could be given. Replies for television are the average for all channels.

It would seem from Table 1 that the viewer expects British television news to be accurate and reliable, but this is not to say that the viewer did not criticize the performance of television during the Gulf War.

All those who were not entirely satisfied with each medium used (i.e. fairly satisfied, or not satisfied) were asked in which ways they were not satisfied and, in the case of television, which channel was involved.

Table 2 is interesting in that the highest complaint against television was not lack of accuracy, bias, lack of trustworthiness or any of the sins that politicians detect and throw at the door of television, but that it was too repetitive (43 per cent), and that too much space was devoted to the war (38 per cent). Indeed, television performed very well in terms of providing information, being balanced, being accurate and keeping the viewer up-to-date with what was happening. Where it went wrong was in 'over-selling' the war. Amongst those who registered dissatisfaction with how television covered the war, the general consensus would appear to be that it squeezed the story for everything that it was worth. In short, the charge against television, in so far as the viewer was concerned, was not a political one, but one of 'entertainment' – 12 per cent of those who were dissatisfied were so because coverage of the war disrupted normal programmes.

It would appear that viewers expect television to be accurate in its reportage of news, and that expectation was fulfilled during the Gulf War. In fact, if we overlay Table 3 with Table 2, the finding that very few viewers were concerned with imbalance in Gulf War coverage on television is reinforced. For example, when asked the probing question whether they thought 'any of the television channels at any stage during the Gulf War allowed their own views to creep into their news or current affairs programmes', the majority (58 per cent) said 'no'. Forty per cent did feel that this had happened; however, among these, one in two said they approved or did not mind, while half disapproved. These results are shown in greater detail in Table 3 for the individual channels.

Table 3. Television channels' own views

	BBC1	BBC2	ITV	C4	Sky	CNN
'Allowed their views to creep into their news or current affairs programmes?'						
NO	75	85	79	87	88	81
YES	25	15	21	13	12	19
'How do you feel about this?'						
Approved	2	1	1	1	1	1
Didn't mind	8	6	9	5	6	10
Disapproved	14	8	10	6	6	8
Don't know	1	1	2	1	–	–

Base: Total sample for BBC, ITV and C4.
* For Sky News and CNN, all receivers of Astra (177) and CNN (72) respectively.

Overall, slightly more viewers said they had noticed this 'creeping of views' on the two BBC channels than on other channels, and were also marginally more likely to say they disapproved of this. It is interesting to consider, at this juncture, the point made earlier about expectations; that is, the figures quoted relating to general trustworthiness of the news showed that the BBC scored particularly highly, and it is possible therefore that this high expectation of accuracy lead people in the crisis of war to have especially high demands of the BBC, and it is interesting, if this argument is accepted, that marginally more people disapproved of this occurring on the BBC than on other channels. In other words, the BBC was seen as having a special duty to be impartial.

Among those receiving Sky or CNN, opinions of these channels were little different. However, CNN was the most likely of the two satellite channels to be perceived as allowing its own views to show. This fact is not too surprising, since the US style of editorializing in news is well-established, and is part and parcel of CNN's own approach.

For all channels, however, the great majority of viewers were either not aware of any 'creeping' editorialization, or were not concerned by it. Given the conversations that took place in the course of the group discussions, this finding is not surprising. Indeed, we used the idea of views 'creeping' into news in the survey, rather than a straightforward statement about bias, because it seemed best to capture how viewers in naturalistic conversation viewed the performance of television. That is, they expected the entry of views, especially from reporters who were close to the action, to colour reports; or, perhaps more accurately, they did not believe that emotions could be kept out of reports in covering scenes such as those witnessed at the Amiriya bunker/shelter. This entry of views did not bother them. As one viewer commented: 'I think you cannot help it. You are around them [casualties] aren't you and you cannot help being influenced by the sorrow and the mourning.' In discussing propaganda with viewers in the groups, most prided themselves on being able to spot falsehood. As one man said: 'You know it's [the report] under Iraqi restrictions. You see the hospital and they are saying this man is a civilian, and he has got his pyjamas on back to front, and you can see the green colour of his uniform.' The viewers did not have the disposition of some trusting child:

> I don't think none of the news that we got during the Gulf War was actually just neutral. You can't say anything bad because it was censored by the Iraqis, or censored by our side. And obviously we want to get some propaganda out of what happened, and they want to get the same, so you can't rely on a totally neutral view.

Clearly, the idea of structured bias was not alien to these viewers: they appreciated that there would be official intervention in the news, but television companies themselves were not blamed for this type of bias. However, if they accepted structured bias as the price to pay for following news events in war, they also appreciated the social strain towards bias:

> It's a thin line, isn't it, between trying to present both sides and being totally propaganda for us. Those civilians (in the Amiriya bunker/shelter) should not have been there. I can see what the Iraqis are trying to present. The reporters are there at first hand and can see the bombing for themselves. Its human nature to make it come as a shock. I mean it can't be easy.

The idea of shock news, or playing up the dramatic side of what after all was a dramatic story – through being caught up in the emotional turmoil of the situation – did not escape the viewers. After watching the film of bodies being removed from the Amiriya bunker/shelter, one viewer commented on the reporter's eyewitness statement – 'another unrecognizable victim was put into a blanket. I think it was the body of a woman' – by saying, 'Why mention it was a women? It could only have been one or the other.' The objection was that to mention the gender of the victim in such circumstances was to slant the news in a dramatic direction and not make a valid news point.

What such comments show is not just the sophistication of viewers' understanding towards news, but also demonstrates an appreciation of the difficulty that the journalist faces in reporting such events. However, despite the perceived difficulty of the reporter on the spot of not allowing his/her emotions to creep into his/her reports, this did not mean that the viewer considered it permissible for the reporter to abandon any effort at being impartial. Quite a few viewers mentioned the criticism made by the journalist John Pilger on the media for not covering the slaughter of the war more fully. But no viewers considered that journalists should adopt an anti-war value stance. This position was put very clearly by one Northern male viewer:

> Our initial discussion started off by saying we agreed with the moral idea of forces being there – I think if Pilger had his way of showing his footage, or whatever footage he wanted to show, is his way of him saying that we should not be in this conflict. But I don't think he has the right to do that through his footage. He's got to be – I don't want to use the word – but unbiased. And it's got to be left to us to make a judgement, but nonetheless we need to make fair judgement on what we see, and what you're (the moderator) trying to get at is what is that balance. And I don't know what that balance is.

This viewer may not have been able to say what balance is, but he clearly thought he would recognize distinct imbalance.

The fact that the majority of viewers were not dissatisfied with the coverage given by television of the Gulf War, nor considered that it was biased, stems, in part, from a willingness to allow the news, within limits, to occupy the position of being humanly constructed. Not having some political axe to grind, they viewed the news with tolerance. From within such a framework of reception, any editorial colouring that did occur was not viewed to be of such prominence as to be worthy of categorizing as interference (bias) in the relay of events that they presumed had actually occurred.

THE VALUES HELD

It is the expectations that viewers have of the news that influence how they judge it, and clearly the expectations that the British viewer has of television news – but not always the press – is that it should be accurate, which means that it should, without editorializing, report events and happenings in the most truthful manner possible. But also, since they see the news as being made by people, they take into account in judging whether the news is fair or accurate, the actual reporting situation and difficulties that a reporting situation might entail. Indeed, to say whether or not something is fair only really makes sense if one knows the situation within which fairness is possible. What was obvious, in both the survey and the group discussions, was that the viewer had a very good understanding of the strictures placed on the flow of news – far more so than was the case during the Falklands Conflict.

However, if the expectations they have about the news gears how it is judged, then so do the values which people hold about the events that are the subject of the news. It could well be expected that if viewers vehemently disagreed with Britain waging war on another country, they would not look favourably upon news that appeared to concentrate on a British version of events. Fairness, in other words, is relative to the rights of participants. For example, viewers would not expect television to give air time to a child abuser out of some intellectual sense of balance simply because a social worker had been speaking about the long-term damage that child abuse causes to children. Can the same be said of war? In other words, must television remain impartial towards the various sides in a war when the combatants are held to have different claims to justice for their acts?

Everyone in the sample was asked their opinion on whether 'During war, journalists' impartiality should be suspended and they should emphasize the British side of things'. The answers to this question are given in Table 4a. Quite clearly the majority of viewers (57 per cent) do not think that impartiality ought to be suspended during a war, but 27 per cent did think that reporting ought to give emphasis to the British side. Whilst it is not the case that the nation is split on the question of impartiality during war, it is not united either. In fact, it is sufficiently divided to present real problems for television, should it opt either for strict impartiality or for a strong British perspective. And indeed, one can see why the *Sun* disappointed its own readers more than any other newspaper disappointed its readers, by the manner in which it covered the war – *Sun* readers were no more likely to demand a pro-British stance than the readers of any other newspaper. Thus, when it comes to war reporting, the *Sun* is out of touch with many of its readers. It may be the paper that boasts it supports 'Our boys and girls', but it is questionable how far its readers support the *Sun*. But of course, as we have already seen, the *Sun* newspaper is not bought primarily for its coverage of news, but more for its general entertainment value.

Table 4a
"How much do you agree or disagree with the following statement?"

					Newspaper readership					
	Total Main	Daily Express	Daily Mail	Daily Mirror	The Star	The Sun	Daily Telegraph	The Guardian	Independent	The Times
Sample base	1015	76	108	220	48	199	65	38	38	26
Weighted base	1015	78	110	227	51	202	64	36	34	24

'During war, journalists' impartiality should be suspended and they should emphasize the British side of things'

	Total Main	Daily Express	Daily Mail	Daily Mirror	The Star	The Sun	Daily Telegraph	The Guardian	Independent	The Times
Strongly agree	53	5	5	15	3	9	3	1	1	3
	5%	6%	5%	7%	5%	4%	4%	2%	3%	14%
Agree	218	15	25	47	15	43	14	–	4	5
	22%	20%	23%	21%	29%	21%	22%	–	13%	22%
Neither agree nor disagree	134	10	18	24	7	33	6	5	8	–
	13%	13%	16%	11%	14%	16%	9%	14%	23%	–
Disagree	422	30	52	95	23	78	33	16	15	9
	42%	39%	47%	42%	44%	39%	51%	46%	43%	35%
Disagree strongly	148	16	9	35	3	25	6	14	5	7
	15%	21%	8%	15%	5%	12%	9%	38%	16%	28%
Don't know/not stated	40	1	1	12	1	14	3	–	1	–
	4%	2%	1%	5%	2%	7%	4%	–	3%	–

Base: All respondents.

However, it is one thing to agree with a statement in principle – that the news should remain impartial – and another matter to hold to that principle in the actual event of war. Furthermore, and notwithstanding the fact that only 15 per cent of viewers disagreed strongly that the news should remain impartial, questions of principle, as we have already argued, should always be tested within a context that gives meaning to the principle. That is, one can, in a hazy sense, strike a position, only to alter it once confronted by what holding to that position involves. The fact, therefore, that the majority of viewers wished for the news to remain impartial ought to be taken, at least for the moment, as no more than an ideological position on how the news ought to perform according to some principled understanding of the role of the 'press' in an open society. Indeed, impartiality, tested to the full during war, appears to be a socially shared value; that is, it is not the preserve of any political grouping as Table 4b shows, but one which is part of the sediment of British values.

Table 4b
"How much do you agree or disagree with the following statement?"

	Politics				
	Conservative	Labour	Soc & Lib/SDP	Green	Other
Sample base	290	280	119	20	26
Weighted base	286	291	120	18	25

'During war, journalists' impartiality should be suspended and they should emphasize the British side of things'

	Conservative	Labour	Soc & Lib/SDP	Green	Other
Strongly agree	14	20	5	1	1
	5%	7%	5%	4%	3%
Agree	66	66	28	2	4
	23%	23%	23%	8%	16%
Neither agree nor disagree	43	26	10	1	3
	15%	9%	8%	5%	11%
Disagree	128	127	54	8	13
	45%	44%	45%	44%	51%
Disagree strongly	30	40	20	7	3
	10%	14%	17%	39%	12%
Don't know/not stated	6	12	4	–	2
	2%	4%	3%	–	7%

Base: All respondents.

What this means is that the idea of fairness operates as a boundary condition on the news. It does not mean that in the situation of war the news must always remain absolutely impartial because, as already argued, whether impartiality or balance is extended to participants in a dispute or event depends on the perceived rights of the participants, or the perceived justice of the participants' case. 'Boundary condition', therefore, refers to a frame of fairness that viewers have towards the news, but which is negotiable depending on the rights of the participants. Thus, the fact that the majority of viewers considered that the news should be impartial during a war can be taken as a firm commitment to the idea of impartiality, but at the same time reflects a commitment that is, in actual operational terms, sufficiently elastic to be stretched or contracted depending on the rights of the participants. This flexibility does not mean that the commitment to impartiality is a kind of moveable feast that constantly shifts to suit the vagaries of an individual's support for some position, person or stance. The commitment to impartiality is solid and impartiality is a solid state which means that the editor cannot move, in his or her treatment of acts and persons, beyond the boundaries of rights that viewers accord to acts and persons. It also means, because of the commitment to the general principle of fairness, that even where the participant in an event is perceived to have very little right on his or her side, the editor cannot totally disregard the notion of impartiality. In such situations balance does not have to be perfect, but both sides of the scales, if not level, must at least be off the ground. Where the participant is seen to have no rights, then the concept of fairness or balance does not come into play at all. In the case of an interview with a child molester, for example, not only might outright dismissiveness of the person's position prove likely to be acceptable to the viewer, but it might be seen as fair.

To understand the reception of the news during the Gulf War, and viewers' appreciation of how the war was reported, we must understand the values that viewers brought to the scenes that they witnessed.

THE NEED FOR WAR

One thing is certain: the British viewer is no pacifist. But that does not mean that he/she supports war under any circumstances. As Table 5 shows, practically everyone agreed that it is acceptable for a country to use armed force against another to defend itself from outside attack – 91 per cent agreed, and only 4 per cent disagreed; the remaining 5 per cent either did not know or considered it dependent on circumstances. However, less than half (47 per cent) considered it right to use armed force against another country to stop that country from making threats against its neighbours, and just over a quarter (28 per cent) considered it acceptable for a country to use armed force against another country to protect its own economy from collapse.

13

Table 5. Opinions on the use of armed force
The use of armed force by one country against another is:

	Yes %	No %	It depends %	Don't know %
Acceptable when a country has to defend itself against outside attack	91	4	4	1
Acceptable for stopping a country's leadership from attacking its own people	51	28	17	4
Acceptable for stopping a country from making threats against its neighbours	47	34	17	2
Acceptable when a country has to protect its economy from collapse	28	52	15	5

Base: Total main sample (1015).

Given that the war in the Gulf involved one country (Iraq) invading another country (Kuwait), and given that Kuwait as an oil supplier has importance to the Western economies, such responses are interesting when held against the fact that 85 per cent of the British public agreed, when the coalition forces attacked the Iraqi armed forces on 17 January 1991, that 'the time had come to use armed force'.

Part of the reason for the belief in the use of armed force to eject Iraq from Kuwait was that most people did not think that the continuation of sanctions would have the desired effect. For example, at the time when the United Nations first imposed sanctions against Iraq six months before the war, 63 per cent did not consider that the situation would be resolved peaceably, and by the time that the United Nations authorized the use of armed force against Iraq, the percentage who believed that armed force would be necessary to force Iraq out of Kuwait had risen to 72 per cent.

Such figures, although demonstrating support for the war, do not provide any feel for how just people thought the war was, nor any expression of depth of feeling about the rightness of going to war. For that we must turn to the group discussions.

Practically all viewers in the group discussions believed, following the United Nations resolution demanding Iraq's withdrawal from Kuwait under the threat of force should Iraq not comply, that war was bound to happen. They did not consider Iraq would withdraw, nor did they believe that if given longer to work sanctions would be effective in getting Iraq to withdraw from Kuwait. Such beliefs, furthermore, did not appear to be influenced by what actually did happen. Their belief that war would follow the United Nations resolution was based on reason and their own understanding of political events. As one Northern man commented: 'I thought war would happen, yes, because I didn't think sanctions would work'. When asked why, he replied, 'Because there are a number of people that break these sanctions aren't there? Stuff was going in through the back door.' Pressed, and asked if he thought sanctions should have been given a longer trial before armed force was used to eject the Iraqis, he replied: 'No. I feel that sanctions would have taken a long time to work and in that time of course atrocities would still be committed against the Kuwaitis.' Another member of the group added: 'I thought it would result in war and I was in favour of going in and getting it sorted out quickly.' There was general agreement for this position: 'They left it too long, I think, because Kuwait was getting hammered.'

The belief that sanctions would not work in this instance was based on the ineffectuality of sanctions as a system when set against known practices of other states in not keeping to instructions. People do not come to situations cold, and a few viewers, based on what they saw as the failure of sanctions to work in the case of South Africa, had a low opinion of sanctions as a political weapon. Thus, working from their own historical understanding of the workings of the world, viewers established likely outcomes of events, not necessarily by what they were told, or what speculations they heard, but by what they, as reflective individuals with their own canons for establishing likelihoods and truths, understand.

We have already seen that some viewers considered that war was inevitably based on the fact that sanctions as a method of imposing political will is flawed, but others came to the same conclusion by a different judgemental working. Quite a few people thought that war was bound to happen because of the psychological make-up of the participants to the dispute. Much blame was placed on Iraq for what one viewer called its 'Death and Glory attitude': 'I think partly them sort of people haven't got the same appreciation of life as we have got.' 'After he [Saddam Hussein] went so far there was no way he could turn back without losing face.'

One of the main reasons for the lack of belief in the effectiveness of sanctions as a way of forcing Iraq to withdraw from Kuwait was the estimation viewers made of Saddam Hussein's personality. One young woman from the North said: 'I didn't think sanctions would work, not with a man like that. Absolute maniac.' Although much was made in the British popular press about Saddam Hussein's mental state, there was

15

no real evidence in the group discussions that viewers actually thought of Saddam as clinically mad. Sometimes he was described as mad, or as a maniac, but mostly it seemed that such terms were used out of a sense of disbelief that someone could behave as he did. In other words, the way the viewers applied the term 'mad' to Saddam's thinking and personality was more akin to the everyday use of the term to capture extreme unreasonableness in someone, or to describe behaviour that could not readily be explained other than by reference to individual oddity. Indeed, it was not just that Saddam Hussein was seen as mad, or difficult to understand, but that culturally the whole of the Middle East was seen as strange. One middle class man from the North made the anthropological judgement that it was very difficult to understand the political manoeuverings of the Middle East because, 'We are trying to judge these things on the standards that we understand. We don't understand Arab and Middle East politics. They are quite different. If we say something we usually mean it.'

Basically, Iraq failed to establish any credibility as a source of trusted information. But in terms of believing that a war was virtually inevitable, cultural differences for most of the viewers were translated as cultural strangeness that propelled the Iraqis to disregard sanctions and the threat of force. As one young man from the Midlands expressed it:

> They have a weird mentality, I think. The way they turn everything into a holy war style against Muslims and against Israel and all that sort of stuff. They kill each other like flies and then expect them to join forces and go and sort everybody else out – crazy. They have got a crazy mentality to me – cannot understand them at all.

One factor that the viewers simply could not come to terms with, and which fostered their distrust of Saddam, was that 'He has murdered and tortured people, women and children. His own people, Iraqis.'

It was Saddam Hussein's perceived readiness to kill 'his own people' that more than anything placed him in a special category of leaders who would do anything to further their own interests, and who was therefore unlikely to respond to anything other than brute force to leave Kuwait which made most viewers consider that war was inevitable.

JUSTICE OF THE WAR AND FAIR REPORTING

The British viewer clearly considered the war with Iraq as inevitable and did so because of estimations of Saddam Hussein's personality. The inevitability of war, however, does not make the waging of war just. Yet the cause of the war, or more precisely the reasons why the United Nations resolution demanding withdrawal was agreed to, was not seen to rest on some single factor such as the committing of a moral wrong by Iraq.

Whilst viewers considered that even if sanctions had been given longer to run, war was not likely to have been averted by sanctions, it did not follow that they considered that the coalition forces arranged themselves against Iraq purely as a result of some high moral ideal. It was seen as wrong that Iraq invaded Kuwait, and right that the coalition forces attacked Iraq, but most viewers considered that the battle in many ways was about oil. When asked what the allies' reasons were for using force, one middle class Midland man summed up the feelings of many when he replied: 'Because of the need for oil. They didn't want to have to answer to Saddam Hussein for nothing.' When other members of the group were asked if the reasons had been based on moral grounds, back came the reply, 'Not the basic reason. It probably came over as that – a moral reason.' This viewer then made the observation, 'You can't sort of go into anywhere without a moral reason really. I mean you just can't go in.'

In discussing with women in the South of England the reason for using force, oil was mentioned as the main drive to resolve the situation. When asked if they considered there were moral grounds for the use of force, one women commented, 'we would like to think so.' This feeling was echoed more fully by a viewer from the North:

> I like to think the reasons are moral. I don't like to think it was about oil. If it had happened in a different part of the Middle East where oil isn't an important issue, I wonder whether the same action would have been taken. But nevertheless I like to think they were moral, and, given that moral standpoint, I think the right decision was made. What I think justifies the loss of life is the threat of power by one person over another.

And one women said:

> I don't think it was just about oil. I think that was a major factor, but they (the Americans) have got a sense of right haven't they? It was the thought of after Kuwait what country would be next, which from what I understand is how we went into the Second World War as well. I mean Poland didn't have any oil as far as I know.

Had the war been seen to be only about oil, it would have been much harder for people to have accepted the adoption of armed force to solve the dispute. There was no doubt, however, that practically all viewers considered the war morally justified. But that did not mean that they thought the war was fought for purely moral principles. As the two viewers suggested above, to believe one had moral rightness on one's side helped them accept the need for war even though the point of the battle was about the control of oil. Indeed, only the most simplistic of minds would combine the reason for war into some single bold category such as a fight against evil. Furthermore, even though viewers considered the control of oil to be a prime reason for the allies taking the stance that they did, they did not necessarily see an economic reason for war as being a wrong reason. Economic reasons for war can also possess a moral dimension. According to one women, 'I had this argument with my husband. He said what right have we got to touch their oil, and Kuwait are selling oil to us cheap and Iraq does not want that.' Her counterargument was: 'Basically we are getting to a stage where the world's resources are going to have to belong to everybody or nobody, and especially not someone as irrational as him [Saddam] controlling it. Yes, I think we had to go in.'

Thus the fact that viewers considered that a primary reason for using force to eject the Iraqis from Kuwait was one of economic interest in having 'friendly' access to oil, did not diminish viewers' belief that it was right for the coalition forces to use military might to exert their demands. The point that left-wing critics of the war overlooked in their denunciations of the use of arms to enforce economic interests, and in their strident attempts to point out to the public that the war was about oil and not moral principles, is that the public accepted that the war was about oil, but still supported armed intervention. Indeed, given that Kuwait was awash with oil, and viewers' knowledge that oil is a vital ingredient to the health of Western economies, it is hardly surprising that oil as a factor in the reason for resorting to armed aggression had not escaped them. As one viewer succinctly put it: 'Bush's motives were because he wanted his fifty pence a gallon for his bloody eight litre cars. That's the bottom of it.' Or as one women commented: 'If Kuwait had produced olive oil, there wouldn't have been a war.'

Thus, whilst the economic reasons for the war did not pass the viewers by, far from it in fact, the point of the war for them, and hence their support, was basically one of morals or rights – the wrongness of one country to overrun another country without good justification. Viewers were genuinely shocked at what Iraq had done to Kuwait, and Saddam Hussein was seen to have a parallel with an earlier dictator: 'He was like Hitler. He didn't care. I mean the way he treated people', was the comment made by one Northern youth. And commenting on those who protested at the war, one women said:

These people that were campaigning against the war – they forget the whole point of why the war was on anyway. About the dreadful things that were done to the Kuwait people. Obviously nobody wanted the war, and nobody wanted anybody hurt, whoever they are, but the people ... they were innocent people that were just invaded by this dreadful man, and his people had no say in what they were doing. He was just a dictator and if they did not do what he told them to do he would just do away with them.

What we see in this woman's obvious anger at the treatment meted out to the Kuwaiti people by the invading forces of Iraq is a concentration on that which she can most clearly grasp – human suffering and wickedness. Most viewers did see a primary reason for the war being about the control of oil, but what engaged their emotions and made them believe the war was worth fighting, was the perceived atrocious behaviour of Iraq. And it was this perceived behaviour and consequently negative moral judgement on Iraq, that had robbed Iraq of the sympathy of British viewers.

In such a situation, British television does not have to be strictly balanced – indeed, on the reasoning made, to achieve a sense of fairness it would be wrong to treat the conflict in the same way as reporting a domestic event involving warring political factions. British television did not, in an attempt to achieve fairness or balance, in so far as the viewers were concerned, have to search out the Iraqi point of view on events. For example, although most viewers (67 per cent) considered it good that British and American journalists were present in Iraq during the war (29 per cent considered it bad, with 4 per cent unsure) their appreciation of such a presence was not based on any particular desire for balance, as Table 6 shows. Only 10 per cent of the reasons given for approving of British journalists in Iraq were because it 'gave both sides' to the war – although 10 per cent of reasons given for approving of journalists in Iraq were 'putting different views across'. The overwhelming reason for approval (35 per cent) was that by having British journalists in Iraq, the viewer in Britain was better informed about the war than had a British contingent not been present. The second highest reason (18 per cent) given by those who approved of British journalists reporting from the enemy country, was that their presence 'brought events home'. In other words, it was not balance, in the accepted media understanding of that concept, that the viewer wanted, but information that was as accurate as possible in the context of the situation within which the journalists had to operate. Fairness, in the sense of providing an Iraqi perspective, was not what was wanted. What was wanted was fair reporting in the sense of accurate reporting. And it is for that reason that the presence of British journalists in the enemy country was appreciated: it was believed that their presence allowed the presentation of a more total picture than would have been the case had they not been there.

If we turn to the group discussions and the response of viewers to the showing of the destruction of the Amiriya bunker/shelter in the sub-urbs of Baghdad, we can bring to life much of the reasoning drawn from the statistics presented above.

The groups were shown recordings of the news reporting of a key incident in the war: the strike on the Amiriya shelter/bunker on the 13 February. BBC, ITN and TF1 reports from their main late evening bulletins were chosen. Viewers were also shown the raw footage from the television news agency, WTN, that they would not have seen. These pictures were much more horrific than any broadcast on British screens.

As soon as the first presentation was over, members were simply asked: What was your reaction to that? To open with the older viewers from the North: 'What's my reaction to it? People get killed. In war people get killed.' Feeling somewhat abashed by the clarity of his statement, this viewer quickly added, 'I'm sorry I said that like I did', to which another, coming to his support, said, 'No, but it's true. People get killed.' As if to justify the lack of sentimentality about the death of others, someone else explained the reasoning behind the responses:

> He [Saddam] put them there. The allies knew, must have known, what
> kind of place it was and he put them there – whether he did it deliber-
> ately or not. It happens. It happened in this country during the second
> world war. And in Germany in the Second World War.

Adding more understanding to their position, another man stated, 'It's part of the thing, isn't it, its part of the game.' And then, as if to demonstrate he fully understood the nature of the game, he added, 'We had British soldiers that were killed accidentally didn't we?'

When asked if they found the scene distressing, not all agreed that they did, but most said 'yes'. One viewer said, 'The Middle Eastern grief is a bit above what we would show', although he had already agreed that he was not upset. Another added:

> I think it's distressing seeing something of that order. I mean let's face
> it, I think you've got to, but my reaction is I think we gave – well overall
> we gave far too much footage to the Iraqis if you like, and we didn't
> show anything of what was happening to the old Kuwaitis – all the
> atrocities that were going on there. We didn't balance it off.

Someone else agreed, and then added, 'I think it was right in this instance to have reported it, but not to have gone into ... not to have made a meal of it as it was done.'

A few points are worth noting here, not least the idea of balance. But the most interesting point is that, because they agreed with the decision to use armed force, they were not about to blame the allied forces for the killing and injuring of Iraqi civilians. They supported the war, and they understood what war was about and, therefore, very rationally from their point of view, they saw little point in being shocked by what they saw. Of course one might see the point of destruction and still be shocked, but what protected these men from too emotional a response was that the deaths and injuries were seen as the misfortunes of war. And to demonstrate their understanding of what does occur in war, and what might be expected, they used the accidental killing of British soldiers by the Americans – they did not blame the Americans, but saw such deaths as very much of the same order as the deaths of the Iraqi civilians. No one was morally culpable, apart from Saddam Hussein who, as far as the viewers were concerned, was responsible for the war, and therefore for all suffering that followed.

Such reasoning protects the emotions. But one of the most important media points is that because all blame for what happened was placed at the door of Saddam Hussein, viewers in general, not just this group, were not that interested in any kind of investigative searching for the truth about whether the shelter was indeed a shelter or a military bunker. It may have been important to liberal or left-wing critics of the war to establish that some awful calumny had taken place, but not to the general viewer, and as such there was little need for television to tread warily or pay special attention with regard to right or wrongness of the strike. The main news story for the viewer was the destruction of the bunker/shelter, not the establishment of 'responsibility' for the deaths. This was a war story, and not a civil accident involving British Rail. Hence, pictures of the dead and injured, when seen by the viewers, were not accompanied by anger, nor surprised shock that something such as what they saw could happen. Indeed, when the idea of balance was introduced by the viewers – 'we didn't show anything of what was happening to the old Kuwaitis – all the atrocities that were going on there. We didn't balance it off'- it was not used with the idea of balancing coalition acts against Iraqi claims that such acts were wrong, but to add weight to one side; namely, to support the coalition's act of destruction by the demand that pictures ought to have been shown that featured the Iraqi destruction of Kuwait. The viewer's demand, therefore, was not

21

for balance, but for the tipping of the scales to put the act of destruction in what, to him or her, was its meaningful context. One woman said:

> I mean when I watched that – the first time I saw it on the day it hap-pened – I felt anger. The news was saying, look what we have done, isn't it awful? Like that lady said, it is war. I mean it is war. People don't die in little plastic bags all nice and neat. I wasn't particularly proud of war, but that is reality – that people get burned alive, mothers and babies and old men. The news made our forces sort of almost on trial – had they done this dirty deed deliberately, or accidently? I felt really angry and I thought this is war and hopefully it is an accident and won't be repeated. But whose side are they on, the news?

What we see here is not a demand for balance, or impartiality, but fair-ness. And fairness is taken to mean the situating of acts within the wider framework of the war. The news, in so far as these last two viewers were concerned, was unfair if it handled events as a collection of incidents, rather than the outcome of an historical process, the responsibility for which rested with Saddam Hussein. Most people, however, carried with them, as a background frame when viewing pictures, a firm belief in who was ultimately responsible for the suffering that was witnessed, and thus, since their demand was for information about what was hap-pening (see Table 6) did not expect some overall setting or balancing of events. As one man said:

> I was really devastated by that film. I was really proud that they could impartially report that. I mean they [the news] didn't say we [troops] should have been there or we shouldn't have been there. I mean they just reported the facts. When he [Bowen, BBC] said this is not propa-ganda, this wasn't staged for us. This was real people with real grief. I thought it was right. We have to know. We can't be told all the time that we are right because sometimes we are wrong. I don't know whether we were wrong in that instance, but we have got to hope that it was entirely a military target. I mean we have got to trust our gov-ernment, our people, because you know if we can't trust them then who can we trust? At least our television coverage could show us that and show us ... it was appalling.

For many in the group, the benefit of British television carrying scenes that could be considered not to reflect favourably on the war effort was that 'It made you feel that what they reported after that was true because they had shown the other side. They had shown you the Iraqi side.'

Table 6. Reasons for opinions about journalists in Iraq
Journalists' presence is:

A good thing	%	A bad thing	%
Informed people	35	Only reported what Iraqis wanted them to	57
Brought events home	18	Danger to journalists	32
Gave both sides	10	Irrelevant	6
Useful despite censors	10	Other replies (all given by less than 5%)	19
Putting different views across	10	Don't know	9
Could reveal truth when they left Iraq	7		
On the spot reporting	6		
Better than relying on Iraqi reporters	5		
Our journalists can be trusted	5		
Other replies (all given by under 5%)	15		
Don't know	4		
Base size:	684		294

CENSORSHIP

Whatever political criticisms were made against British television for reporting from an enemy country, it is clear from the above statements that one of the effects was to increase the credibility of the news to British viewers. It was not, however, as if the British viewer was unaware of the reporting restrictions that were placed on the journalists in Iraq. Indeed, Table 6 shows that the main reason given by those viewers who objected to the presence of British and American journalists in Iraq was because they 'could only report what Iraqis wanted them to', but Table 7 shows that despite the viewers' belief in a high degree of restrictions being imposed on British journalists in Iraq, 20 per cent of the sample still trusted the reports 'a lot'. However, as Table 7 shows, the degree of restrictions placed on journalists with the coalition forces was seen as much less than that imposed on journalists in Iraq, with a consequently higher level of trust placed in reports from the coalition front – 41 per cent of the sample, trusted them 'a lot'.

Yet, even though a fairly high degree of scepticism existed towards the reports from the Iraqi theatre of operations, the fact that the reports could not be accepted at face value did not overly bother the viewers in the group discussions. They saw themselves as individuals who were extremely media literate and prided themselves on being able to sift false information from true information. Furthermore, it was not as if they suspended their critical faculties when examining news originating from the coalition front – they were simply more likely to consider that what they had been told had a greater chance of being true than the information emanating from Iraq. And, as we have seen, the fact that British television showed the destruction of the Amiriya bunker/shelter helped foster the feeling that the British media and authorities were not attempting to hide unpleasant, and perhaps unfavourable, facts.

Table 7. The relative effects of censorship

	Journalists in Iraq %	Journalists with coalition %
'How restricted were they in what they could say?'		
Highly restricted	48	19
Fairly restricted	39	59
Not very restricted	7	13
Not restricted at all	3	2
Not sure/Don't know	6	7
'Overall, how much did you trust the reports?'		
Trust a lot	20	41
Trust a little	40	47
Not trust much	26	9
Not trust at all	13	2
Don't know	1	1

Base: Total sample.

The question of censorship is another area of questioning, like fairness, that can only be handled by placing it in some kind of context that allows the viewer to make a decision based on specific information. That is, it is pointless asking whether someone is for or against censorship without providing specific instances where censorship might be applied. Without knowing what is to be censored, the viewer cannot make a moral judgement about the right or wrong of denying information to the public. However, before examining concrete instances of where censorship or collusion in carrying false information might come into being, it is worth noting that most viewers do not demand a 'flow of consciousness news' such as that proffered at times by CNN. For example, when asked, 'What do you think is the most important thing in reporting an event during a war – reporting an event at the time that it happens, or reporting it only when all the details are clear?' – 67 per cent of viewers wished for events to become 'news' only when the picture of what had occurred became clear. Twenty per cent, however, did wish for instantaneous reporting, with a further 11 per cent undecided.

This preference for the journalist to act as an intelligent gatherer of information, where he or she imposes his/her own understanding on events before offering an editorial judgement to the viewer about what has taken place, rather than acting as a messenger of what they are seeing, suggests a viewer that is willing to forgo immediate information for the sake of a broad vista of understanding. The viewer does not, in other words, wish for unfiltered 'news'. But equally, the viewer does not expect, at least in a war situation, that all information that is known will be relayed to them. And it here that we come into the area of moral judgement and values.

A series of questions was put to viewers concerning not just censorship, but the role of journalists in carrying information in time of war. Asked whether news media should 'deliberately put out false information in the hope that it would help win the war', the majority of viewers disagreed with such collusion – 66 per cent disapproved, 23 per cent approved and 11 per cent had no opinion. It would appear that the British viewer does not wish for the fourth estate to become the fourth service, but when the context became that of carrying false information to save the lives of British troops, the position is almost reversed as Table 8 shows.

The fact that only 14 per cent of viewers thought that a journalist should refuse to give out false information to save British lives, may, without reflection, suggest that the British public has scant regard for the democratic principle of open reporting. On further examination, however, the fact that the majority of viewers (64 per cent) wished for the truth to be broadcast once the war was over, reveals a public very much committed to truth, at least historically. That is, the public does not wish for a lie to go uncorrected, once the strategic reason for falsehood has passed. Faced with a genuine moral decision – commitment to truth at the cost of human life – the public is not prepared to accept that journalists have the right to put professional practice – the canon of telling the truth – above all other considerations.

Table 8. Opinions on how journalists should act
"If the army asked a British journalist to give out a false report to confuse the enemy thus saving a lot of British lives, which of these comes closest to what you think the journalist should do?"

	%
Give a false report and then keep the fact secret even after the war	17
Give a false report but reveal the truth once the war was over	64
Do not give false report at all	14
Don't know	4

By and large, however, the public did wish to be told the truth about events, even if that truth was 'negative'. In the scenarios shown below, there was no context given involving direct threat to British forces, and the majority in three of the four scenarios felt that if a journalist made such discoveries he/she should report the information even whilst the war was in progress (see Tables 9, 10, 11 and 12).

Table 9. Reporting of negative events
"If a British journalist discovered British troops mistreating Iraqi prisoners of war, which of these comes closest to what you think he should do?"

	%
Attempt to report it while war going on	69
Only report it once war over	21
Never report it even after the war	6
Don't know	4

Table 10. Reporting of negative events
"... a British journalist in Baghdad has seen several coalition planes shot down. A true report has been given on Baghdad radio. The journalist has been asked to report lower figures to help keep up morale at home. Should he report the true figure or not?"

	%
Yes, report true figure	66
No, report false figure but reveal truth once war has ended	25
No, report false figure and never reveal truth even once war is over	4
Don't know	5

Table 11. Reporting of negative events
"If a British journalist discovered that casualties among coalition forces had been caused by other coalition forces and not by the enemy, should he report this?"

	%
Yes, while war is going on	72
Yes, but only after war	20
Never report it even after war	5
Don't know	3

Table 12. Reporting of negative events
"If the war was going badly due to a mistake on the part of the commanders, should a British journalist report this mistake?"

	%
Yes, while war is going on	44
Yes, but only after war	42
Never report it even after war	10
Don't know	4

It therefore seems to be the case, judging from the various scenarios, that the principle to which most people adhere – truthful and open reporting – can become modified by the context in which journalists have to make decisions. Where there are no direct consequences – such as threat to British life – the principle is 'publish' (Tables 9, 10 and 11). Where there is a risk, the principle is amended to retrospective truth-telling. This can be seen in Table 12, where the reporting of mistakes by commanders should not be shown, according to many, whilst war is in progress.

THE WILLINGNESS TO WITNESS

Much fuss is made of censorship, or the placing of restrictions on reports during war, but what we have seen is that the viewer does not have an absolute position in terms of what material should be carried and what should not be carried; rather a set of judgements which he/she applies in determining what he/she should be told, of which the basic rule would appear to be that material that is likely to damage the war effort, but in particular risk lives, has a higher claim for restricted release than material that might simply prove embarrassing to military and political authorities. As important as this finding is, very little attention, in the past, has been paid to what the viewer wishes to see of the images of war. Do viewers wish to be protected from the absolute horrors of war, or do they wish for detailed shots of the dead and injured? How far, in other words, should editors edit footage to remove graphic scenes of destruction and injury that occur in the course of military conflict?

To begin with we chose four specific events in the war, and asked everyone in the sample to say whether or not such incidents should have been carried by British television. The ones selected were all given wide coverage: the bombing of a bunker/shelter in Baghdad that resulted in heavy civilian casualties; the coalition pilots captured by Iraq and displayed on Iraqi television broadcasts; the filming of Iraqi troops surrendering; and the aftermath of coalition air attacks on Iraqi forces as they were withdrawing from Kuwait along the road to Basra in the final days of the conflict. Not only did these events attract widespread coverage, but also considerable debate as to the morality and acceptability of each. The four situations were asked about in a different order in each individual interview, ensuring that any particular one did not unduly influence replies for the remainder.

Majorities of viewers said that they had seen television coverage of these events; 73 per cent saw coverage of the bombing of the Amiriya bunker/shelter in Baghdad, 85 per cent saw the captured coalition pilots, 75 per cent saw pictures of Iraqi troops surrendering, and 57 per cent recalled seeing coverage of the results of air attacks on Iraqi troops on the road to Basra. In each case, all those who said they had seen television coverage were further asked whether it had been right or wrong to show this on British television.

For three of the four, most people thought it had been right to show these on television. However, in the case of the transmission of Iraqi film showing captured coalition pilots – including two Britons – the majority view was that this should not have been shown (Table 13).

Table 13. Opinions on television coverage of specific events

	Bunker bombing %	Captured pilots %	Iraqi PoWs %	Attack on Basra road %
Right to show	72	40	78	80
Wrong to show	23	57	16	14
Don't know	5	3	6	6
Unweighted base:	737	863	763	579

Note: Per cent based on those saying they had seen television coverage of each specific event.

The reasons given by viewers for saying that it was right to show coverage of these events centred mainly around showing the truth about war – what war is like, reminding people that war causes casualties, and the need to show both sides. In the case of the captured pilots, the simple fact that the coverage showed them to be alive was felt by a sizeable minority to be a good reason in itself. However, there were also other reasons given which were not connected with the 'morality' of war or its reporting; sizeable proportions of viewers felt that showing Iraqis in a poor light was a good reason for having such coverage (Table 14).

Table 14. Reasons for televising specific events

	Bunker bombing %	Captured pilots %	Iraqi PoWs %	Attack on Basra road %
Shows what war is really like	55	37	22	53
The truth should always be shown	37	29	18	35
Showed prisoners to be alive	–	28	–	–
Gave a balanced view of both sides in war	16	–	–	14
Reminded people that civilians are casualties as well as soldiers	20	–	–	7
Showed Iraq using civilians to disguise bunker/Iraqi cruelty/unwilling to fight	10	24	44	–
Showed British/coalition forces brave/kind	–	28	14	–
Shows humanity of both sides	–	–	14	–
Showed power of coalition forces/ruthlessness	7	–	–	23
Other (under 5 per cent)	8	10	11	14
Unweighted base:	534	345	593	466

Base: Those saying it was right to show TV coverage of each. All replies given verbatim and coded after interview.

In contrast, the reasons given by those who felt it was wrong to show these items on television concentrate either on the potential risk of upsetting people – both adults and children – or upon the perceived propaganda and negative morale impact of coverage. Also, the specific example of the captured coalition pilots can be seen to be quite different from the other three; the main reason given was that the relatives of the airmen shown would be upset (Table 15).

If we take the two 'horror' incidents of the war that were shown on British television – the bunker/shelter bombing and the attack on the Basra road – what is noteworthy is that the main reason given for not showing such incidents is 'upsetting for adults' – the bunker/shelter scores only marginally more as a propaganda event for Iraq (Table 15). However, if we examine Table 14 the major reason given for why it was right to show these two incidents was, it 'shows what war is really like'.

On the one hand, therefore, the portrayal of scenes of death and injury are approved of because it shows the true face of war, but on the other hand they are objected to because such scenes upset people. These responses, although ostensibly standing in opposition to each other, ought to be seen as a product of asking people to make a definite judgement about what should be shown and what should not be shown, and whilst revealing distinct groupings of attitudes, nevertheless, as many survey questions do, serve to hide the common feelings that apparently opposing respondents often share with each other. That is, for the minority who did not want the pictures of the destruction of the bunker, or the attack on the fleeing Iraqis, to be shown on television for the reason, in the main, that they would upset viewers, it does not mean that they disagreed with those who supported showing such pictures on television on the grounds that the true face of war ought to be brought to the attention of the watching public. If Table 15 is examined closely, one of the main reasons given for not approving of the bunker/shelter scene, and the road to Basra scene, was that they considered that they had enough imagination to grasp what had taken place without the need for detailed visual representation. It is not, therefore, that they did not wish to know about what went on in war, but rather that they disagreed about what it was neccessary to screen to establish that fact. And it is not sufficient to argue that the viewer needed the pictures to establish the true face of war, because what was shown – and this applies to what is actually shot in any war – did not and could not visually capture the total permutations of death and injury, never mind the experiences of those caught up in the run of battle.

Table 15. Reasons for *not* televising specific events

	Bunker bombing	Captured pilots	Iraqi PoWs	Attack on Basra road
	%	%	%	%
Let Iraqis stage a propaganda event	32	21	11	16
Upsetting for adults	29	14	20	25
Upsetting for children	24	9	12	21
Don't need to see it/can imagine it	21	9	18	23
Undermined British morale	14	2	9	–
Made British feel sorry for Iraqis	10	–	44	12
Showed suffering/degrading/humiliating	9	5	36	1
Upsetting for relatives of victims/prisoners	1	73	19	–
Against rules of war/Geneva Convention	–	21	5	5
Other (under 5 per cent)	7	10	11	25
Unweighted base:	165	491	122	466

Base: All saying it was wrong to show TV coverage of each event. All replies given verbatim and coded after interview.

What we come to, therefore, in so far as television is concerned, is not so much editorial judgement of what should or should not be shown, but what the viewer thinks is neccessary to establish that an event has occurred and what type of event it was. Is it, for example, quite sufficient for the viewer to hear a verbal report that such and such an event has happened, or sufficient to receive a verbal but descriptive account of the event, or is it sufficient to use establishing shots accompanied by a verbal description of happenings, or is it necessary to describe events and happenings accompanied by close-up shots of destruction, injury and death? These were all areas that we tried to explore in both the survey and the group discussions.

A range of questions was included in the survey asking about coverage of events in terms of their acceptability to viewers. The approach adopted in these was to ask about specific events, either ones which happened and which received significant coverage, or to construct detailed scenarios and ask about these. This method was adopted in order to avoid people giving generalized answers, which are of little overall meaningfulness in terms of finding out about the limits of acceptability. Rather, by concentrating on specifics, the effect of context can be assessed, and individuals can also be asked more detailed questions about specific elements within each context.

Three specific scenarios were included in the study. The first was unrelated to the Gulf War, and asked about a serious train crash. The second and third asked about land battles resulting in Iraqi military casualties and British military casualties respectively. For each one, respondents were asked to say which from a range of types of television coverage were acceptable to them. These ranged from the inclusion of pictures of the dead or injured, down to no pictures of casualties, only descriptions being used.

Overall, there are few differences between the patterns of response for the three scenarios. Few were willing to accept close-ups of dead or wounded – although the proportion saying this was acceptable in the case of Iraqi casualties was somewhat greater, though still small, than in the other two cases. In both military scenarios, though, fewer people opted for the 'show only after the dead and injured had been removed' option (Table 16).

Table 16. Acceptable forms of TV coverage of three scenarios

	Serious train crash %	Battle with Iraqi casualties %	Battle with British casualties %
Acceptable for TV to:			
Include close-up pictures of the dead	6	11	8
Include close-up pictures of the badly injured	8	9	7
Only show the scene from a distance so that the faces of the dead are not recognisable	47	42	48
Only show the scene after the dead and badly injured have been removed	43	28	34
Show no pictures of the dead or injured, simply describe the scene	28	28	29
All acceptable	2	2	2
Don't know	2	2	2

Note: Total per cent sum to more than 100 per cent due to multiple replies.

All who said that the dead or injured should be shown in each case were further asked to give their reasons for their choices. It is worth noting the different types of reasons given for the rail crash. In the military scenario, the main reason given was that news should reflect reality. While this was also the most frequently given reason for the two military examples, these also attracted higher levels of responses stressing the need to show the horrors of events, and the damage and casualties that occur (Table 17).

Table 17. Reasons for accepting the showing of casualties

	Serious train crash %	Battle with Iraqi casualties %	Battle with British casualties %
The news should be as close to what actually happened as possible	73	64	62
It gets across the horror of the event	46	51	56
People should be shown the damage caused by this kind of event	37	51	43
It will stop people glorifying war	–	25	28
It will help stop war	–	15	19
It shows the attacks are working	–	9	8
It shows valour and bravery	–	2	4
Base size:	134	192	139

Base: All saying casualties should be shown in each case.

All those who said that pictures of the dead or injured should not be shown, or that no pictures at all should be shown, were also asked to give their reasons for saying this. Overall, the patterns of responses did not differ greatly; upsetting relatives of victims was the most often-given reason (albeit at a lower level for the Iraqi scenario), followed by the dislike of seeing bodies (particularly those of Iraqi soldiers) (Table 18).

Many people also gave other people's likely responses as a reason for not showing the casualties, with the main worry being about the impact of such scenes on children (see later section for evidence of anxiety and children). These fears for children are not particularly the province of parents. Though those of the sample who did have children were more likely to say that children would get upset (43 per cent of those with children aged under 9 and 38 per cent of those with older children), the majority (70 per cent) of those giving this reason were in fact those without children living at home. Relatively few people expressed concern about the possible impact on public morale or the potential propaganda value of casualties being shown.

The above tables help support the argument that was made from Tables 13 and 14, that the difference between those who approved of the showing of the scenes of the destruction of the bunker/shelter and the carnage on the road to Basra were, very likely, not much different from those who did not, in their approval of television showing the true face of war. That is, those who did not approve of the scenes were not arguing that the destruction of war should be kept off the screens, but differed from those who approved only in how reality ought to be represented. What we see now, however, when the question of representation is specifically questioned, is that very few people really wish for the full horror of war to be shown on their screens. As one woman in the group discussions commented to illustrate her objection to the graphic portrayal of war injuries: 'You wouldn't show motorway crashes with people's heads cut off and bodies hanging out of windscreens. We know what a crash is.'

The comment 'we know what a crash is', is the qualitative dimension to the statistical finding in Table 15 of the response 'Don't need to see it/can imagine it', referring to not wanting to see pictures of injury from the attack on the bunker/shelter or the devastation inflicted on the Iraqi troops as they fled down the road to Basra. Yet, examining Tables 17 and 18 there is a suspicion that viewers will accept, at least emotionally, more close-up shots of injury in war than they will in the case of coverage of civilian accidents. Table 17 shows that although the main reason for accepting the showing of casualties is the belief that the news 'should be as close to what actually happened as possible', this was more likely to be given in the case of a train crash than war, whereas for the second most likely reason given – 'it gets across the horror of the event' – the train crash was less likely to be given than the two war situations. Such responses do suggest that the showing of injuries in war has a higher purpose to it than the showing of injuries in civilian accidents. In the latter case the approval of showing casualties is driven by the news demand of covering the story to get across what actually happened, but in the case of the former, especially when the other responses are taken into account, such as 'people should be shown the damage caused by this kind of event', and 'it will stop people glorifying war', it would appear that viewers are saying that there is a justifiable purpose in showing casualties in that they act as a reminder that war has human consequences which politically we ought to confront.

Table 18. Reasons for *not* accepting the showing of casualties

	Serious train crash %	Battle with Iraqi casualties %	Battle with British casualties %
It will upset the relatives of the dead and injured	75	51	74
Don't need to see dead bodies	37	46	37
Children will get upset	33	33	34
We have enough imagination to work it out for ourselves	28	37	36
I don't want my children to see it	23	20	24
Some adults will get upset	20	19	20
Words are better than pictures for telling such stories	11	15	12
Dislike the sight of blood or injury	10	11	13
It makes the viewer feel helpless	10	8	11
It will help enemy propaganda	–	15	12
It will help anti-war protesters	–	10	8
It will make viewers want to stop the attacks	–	4	6
Unweighted base size:	601	489	526

Base: All saying bodies/injured/pictures should not be shown on TV.

Very few people, however, believed that showing scenes of destruction and injury would help stop war. And as further support for this reasoning, Table 18, giving the responses of those who did not accept the showing of casualties, shows that the main reason for not wanting such footage was not that they considered it unnecessary 'to see dead bodies', but that such pictures 'will upset the relatives of the dead and injured'. Their objection to such pictures was out of concern for others, and not because of some emotional resistance to viewing scenes of injury, or failing to support the moral/political lesson that such pictures might deliver. And that is why the scores for both objecting to the showing of casualties of a train crash and British battle casualties are the same, but those for the showing of Iraqi casualties are lower. (Should it be suggested that the lower score reflects a lack of identity with Iraqi soldiers and therefore a lower threshold of acceptance to pictures of injury, then whilst this could be the case, it is unlikely since it would not account for the large difference in response. The differences might have been even larger if it were not for the fact that some viewers, and probably because of CNN, thought that viewers in Iraq were seeing the same pictures as those received by British viewers.)

If we now turn to the group discussion, and people's responses after viewing the showing of the footage of the strike on the Amiriya bunker/shelter, we can see more closely the restrictions that viewers wish to be placed on the images of war.

The showing of film from the BBC, ITN, TF1 and WTN of the human devastation caused by the bombing of the bunker/shelter, produced tensions within the groups, and differences of opinion as to the value of such a broadcast. Nevertheless, practically everyone thought that the BBC and ITN were right to show the footage that they did show, but hardly anyone considered that it would have been correct for ITN to have shown the WTN footage.

The question of what images to show to provide the viewer with a good account of what actually happened was hotly debated by the viewers. The balance of the argument swung between showing sufficient detail to convey the event as actuality, and not showing too much so that it revolted the sensibilities.

The overwhelming vote was that the television companies had got the amount and type of images about right in covering the bunker/shelter story. One woman from the Midlands said: 'I personally think that they showed enough, and you can imagine a certain amount. We all know what's happening. You don't need to look at it.' This was a fairly typical comment. After watching the BBC clip, one older woman from South London commented:

> I think it's very disturbing, but really as adults you should be aware
> of what's going on. I think you have to view in context, and think more

into it. So although it is disturbing and harrowing we could sit here and think of those Iraqis as bad guys with no feelings, and you could become very easy about the whole thing. But seeing that brings home the seriousness of the whole thing.

What the viewers are saying, in effect, is that although the footage was disturbing, the showing of it was justified because it had a point and a purpose to it. The point appeared to be that since an event had taken place, and part of that event was the killing and maiming of civilians, as adult viewers they should not be denied the factual visual element of the story. However, when the WTN footage was shown, which had not been broadcast by ITN on grounds of taste, the tolerance to viewing grue-some pictures was tested to the limit: 'I think they were too much. Keep them out. We know what was going on, it wasn't necessary to show them' was the comment of one South London woman. The shots pro-vided by WTN were of charred bodies, so badly cindered that it was quite difficult to make out the human forms. Such scenes troubled one young man, also from South London: 'It's a very fine line between show-ing that and bad taste. I thought when I was watching it – hold on, I don't want to see any more, I've seen one charred body I don't want to see more. It was just sick, like the cameraman was saying, yea, let's get an-other one in.'

What is interesting is that quite a few of the viewers in the group dis-cussions wished to make a distinction between what was permissible for the news to show, and what was permissible for current affairs pro-grammes and documentaries to show. One woman, who considered that ITN was right not to show the WTN footage, said, 'I think *World in Action* could show it, where you know what it will be like, but not the news.' One man, who had considered the pictures shown by ITN and the BBC were 'strong enough' said, 'I wouldn't want to see nasty things on television – they shouldn't show bloody bodies and corpses, they should be covered up', but he nevertheless considered that the WTN footage would be acceptable, 'possibly on a documentary programme after the war, possibly a couple of days after it had happened.'

This distinction that the viewers made about what detail of injury to show, according to whether it was screened as part of the news or as part of a documentary or current affairs programme, is interesting in that it shows that they wish to be protected from being taken by surprise over what they might see when they switch on the television. It also shows a recognition on the part of the viewer that if such pictures are deemed neccessary to make a document of truth about what took place during the war then such footage ought to be included. Indeed, this evidence, drawn from the group discussions, fits with the statistical findings of the survey, where greater acceptance was made for the release of information after the war was over than when in progress. That is, the viewer did not wish for a restriction to be placed on information, be it print information, voice or picture information, providing there was some justifiable reason for releasing or showing such material. The documentary and the current affairs programme were seen to have a higher claim for including graphic injury in programmes than did the news, because it was presumed that such pictures would be neccessary for the point that the documentary wished to make, or that the detailed nature of the current affairs programme might demand the inclusion of such pictures. But also, and this is the point the woman viewer made, the type of content that a documentary or a current affairs programme was likely to feature could be guessed at in advance by virtue of knowing the topic that was being covered, whereas the rolling nature of news precluded such precise prediction and therefore the editors of news were held to have a responsibility not to present surprise shocks.

However, the actual impact of the pictures, in so far as the viewers were concerned, depended also on the voice reports accompanying them; indeed, viewers were critical of the use of any words that heightened the horror of images that were already considered horrible enough. As one women from the Midlands said, 'It is what you hear that disturbs me, it's not always what you see.' What she objected to was the statement in the report on the Amiriya strike which said – 'At one hospital, staff were trying to arrange the dismembered corpses into something recognisable.' She commented:

> You pick up on dismembered corpses. It has an effect inside. I felt what the commentator was saying. I do not watch horror movies, but those two words instantly brought to me horror movies. You look and you wonder – was that blood? But if the commentator says 'dismembered bodies', it seems to linger on.

Another viewer in the same group said that the phrase 'dismembered bodies' shocked her and even considered that it was worse hearing that phrase than seeing the cindered bodies of the WTN footage. However, she still thought it was right of ITN not to show the WTN shots on the grounds that: 'I cannot see that it was necessary to put it in, so in my opinion it was right to take it out.'

37

What this viewer is saying in effect is that if horrific footage is included in the news, then the television companies must be able to justify its inclusion. That is, simply because the story carried by the news is one of war, does not mean that graphic scenes of death and injury have an automatic place in the news or 'right' to be included. Such footage, in so far as the viewers are concerned, does not have an automatic claim for inclusion because they did not consider that the function of the news was that of making anti-war statements. Its function was seen to be that of relaying what was happening in the war and in relaying what was happening it was not considered necessary for the news to include close up shots of injury, but merely establish that injury had occurred. The viewers value position was that war in itself was not wrong, and that the Gulf War in particular was not wrong.

Sensibilities are not free floating, but are anchored within a moral framework which make acts more or less disturbing. It is one's values that make one sensitive to certain occurrences and not others. Indeed, sensibilities are inseparable from values. And when it comes to the news because the viewer did not wish for a political point to be made about unfortunate consequences of war, viewers' sensibilities were affronted when confronted by graphic scenes of human suffering which they considered went beyond the point of establishing the occurrence of an event.

At no point in any of the group discussions did viewers express a desire for the raw images of war to be kept off their screens. Indeed, some harrowing footage was broadcast, and the viewers considered that it was right to show such scenes. In short, they found the scenes acceptable. But the interesting finding is that throughout the group discussions viewers' sensibilities did appear to be buttressed against outright onslaught by their acceptance of the war as both just, and given the perceived intransigence of Saddam Hussein, inevitable. Basically, blame for all suffering was placed at Saddam Hussein's door, and this fact mediated the impact of the images seen.

It was this framework of understanding and judgement of the war that provided the adult viewer with an emotional shield against any harrowing scenes that they might have seen on television and also helped guard against general anxiety about the war. However, it is one thing for the general viewer to watch and follow the events in the Gulf and sift the material so as not to threaten their emotional and mental stability, but what about children? Did they suffer anxiety as a a result of watching the pictures of the war in the Gulf?

38

To address this question the study took a sample of 212 children, aged 9–15, drawn from the same households as the main adult sample and administered a much shorter and altered version of the adult question-naire to them. However, in order to understand how children talked about the war and the language they used to describe their feelings about and responses to issues, the study also conducted four group dis-cussion with children, two in the South of England and two in the North of England. The results of this part of the study are given in the next section.

2. Children and Anxiety

CHILDREN'S RESPONSE TO THE COVERAGE OF THE GULF WAR

The coverage of the Gulf War, with the 'live' on-the-spot reporting via satellite, helped foster the impression of events being played out in real time rather than the emotionally protective distance of recorded time. Although in actual fact, apart from pictures of Scud missiles being intercepted, hardly any of the action footage seen was live combat, the coverage of the war nevertheless managed to create the feeling of excitement that the war was being reported on a blow-by-blow basis as the events happened. It is interesting that one of the older girls said, 'It's weird to think that when our children grow up and go to school and learn about this war, they'll say to us, were you there, and we'll say, yes, we were there.'

For some of the children in the group discussions this was the first time they had felt any real interest in watching the news. Some children had even taken their Walkmen into school so that they could tune into news bulletins throughout the day; a practice stopped by irate teachers when they discovered the children started to tune into pop music programmes. Even so, it is not surprising, as Table 18 has already shown, that adults were bothered by the prospect of children seeing pictures of casualties on television, and equally not surprising, therefore, that anxiety in children should raise itself as an issue during the Gulf War.

As stated, the questionnaire administered to children was much shorter than the fifty-five-minute one given to adults – ten to fifteen minutes long – and the wording of those questions which were ostensibly the same as in the adult survey was altered to accommodate their age. When asked if they considered it right for Britain to join other countries in war against Iraq, 54 per cent thought it was definitely right to do so, 24 per cent considered it was probably right, with 6 per cent and 7 per cent respectively considering it was probably not or definitely not right to join with other countries in war – 9 per cent were undecided.

Table 19
"Why did you make a point of asking your parents about the Gulf War?"

		Sex		Age	
	Total	Male	Female	9–12	13–15
Sample base	82	41	38	43	37
What was discussed					
Tell them you are worried/fears	9	1	7	5	3
	11%	2%	18%	12%	8%
Ask about politics/history/background	16	8	8	8	6
	20%	20%	21%	19%	16%
Ask about ecology/wildlife/ environment	8	5	3	6	2
	10%	12%	8%	14%	5%
Ask about weapons/equipment used	9	7	1	4	4
	11%	17%	3%	9%	1%
Discuss specific incident seen on television	4	1	3	1	3
	5%	2%	8%	2%	8%
Discuss specific incident heard about on radio	1	–	1	–	1
	1%	–	3%	–	3%
Discuss specific incident talked about in school	2	1	1	–	1
	2%	2%	3%	–	3%
Ask if war is right or wrong	9	3	5	3	5
	11%	7%	13%	7%	14%
Ask about terrorism/threats in Britain/what will happen here	11	3	8	6	5
	13%	7%	21%	14%	14%
Ask about family/friends involved in war/living or working in Middle East	10	6	4	7	3
	12%	15%	11%	16%	8%
Ask what they think will happen	17	12	4	7	9
	21%	29%	11%	16%	24%
Others	2	1	1	2	–
	2%	2%	3%	5%	–

Base: All who have made a point of asking parents about the Gulf War.

There was no doubt who the children considered was responsible for the war – Saddam Hussein. As one young boy said: 'I just remember that he was the one that made this war, and he was the one that killed the people and made our soldiers and Americans kill the innocent people in the air raid shelter and things, and destroy all his buildings. I just think it's him that's made the war.' 'It's all his [Saddam's] fault,' said one

Northern girl, 'he's forcing his own people into war.' In a very certain manner, a young boy from the South summed up his position by saying, 'There's something wrong with him ... they should have dealt with him ages ago, because he's killed a lot of innocent people for no reason ... he's killed a lot of his people and ours.'

The age group of the children ranged from nine years old to fifteen, but what is interesting is that the difference in gender responses between the adult survey and the children's survey shows similar patterns. For example, 74 per cent of adult men agreed 'a lot' with the decision of the coalition forces to attack Iraq when they did, but only 57 per cent of women did. In the children's survey, 62 per cent of boys definitely agreed that it was right for Britain to join other countries in war against Iraq, but only 44 per cent of girls did. It would certainly look as if attitudes to war have a gender dimension that is structured fairly early on in life. It would also appear, however, that the girls were more anxious about the war than were the boys. When the children were asked if they had made a point of asking their own parents about the war, 39 per cent said they had, of which 42 per cent were girls and 35 per cent boys. When given the open-ended question asking them why they asked their parents about the war, 18 per cent of girls who had questioned their parents said it was to talk about their own fears and worries, compared to only 2 per cent of boys (Table 19).

The bases for these responses are, given the overall sample size, low, and of course, the raising of worries by girls cannot on its own be taken as representing a higher index of anxiety than that shown by boys: it may be that boys did not wish to confess to anxiety.

The one area about which the children in the group discussion did express anxiety was terrorism, especially those children talked with in the South of England who lived close to Heathrow airport. The threat of terrorism seemed more real to them than it did to the children in the North. As one youngster from the Leeds area commented: 'Only top people get blown up, and they all live in London.' In fact, although at the outbreak of the war the children in the group discussions confessed to being worried about the possibility of terrorist raids by Iraq, that fear receded when no such terrorist activity happened: 'At the beginning of the war like you're always aware that terrorists could attack, but not now, now you're not so worried because like it's gone on for quite a long time and you're not so worried because they haven't attacked yet. Why should they?' 'I never actually thought they'd actually bring planes out here and bomb us. Well, I did at the beginning, but then I thought no. Have to refuel too much.' The terrorism that did worry them was terrorism by the IRA, but that worry predated the Gulf War. It seemed more like a running concern, fuelled by stories on television about IRA activity.

Their fear, however, was not for the safety of themselves, but rather for the safety of their family, mainly their parents.

> You're scared that somebody might shoot somebody in your family or something like that – like the IRA shot down a man when it was his daughter's birthday party. He just opened the door and they just shot him down.

> I think about the IRA a lot because what if they came over here and got my dad and got him by accident like those two Australian men which were got accidently.

> You never think they are going to get your mum, it's always your dad. I don't know why but you always think they're going to get your dad if they're going to get anybody. If they got you, you wouldn't be the one left to be upset, but if your dad died .... .

The above quotes concerning worry over the IRA are taken from the girls groups and it would be wrong to suggest, since group discussions have their own dynamic in following specific issues, that girls show a higher degree of anxiety about terrorist attacks on their family than do boys, but from the above figures relating to conversations with their parents about their worries prompted by the Gulf War, whilst not necessarily showing a higher level of anxiety in girls than boys, it nevertheless does appear that girls demonstrated a degree of uncertainty about the war which, like all uncertainty, provides ready ground for anxiety. It may be that the girls in the sample had a more 'open' or confiding relationship with their parents than did the boys, but that would not account unduly for the type of issues that they wished to discuss. It would seem that their less ready acceptance of war may have been at the root of such questions. And it is interesting that, when children were asked if their parents had made a point of talking to them about the war, of the 36 per cent who said they had, there was no difference between the sexes.

Of course, it is always difficult to say who initiates a conversation, and such self-reportage, as opposed to observation, ought not to be too strongly relied upon as a base upon which to ground statements about anxiety: it might be well to challenge the assumption that the points the girls talked about with their parents is evidence of anxiety when the parents themselves – always presuming that they accept the assumption that talk is good for reducing anxiety and not the other way around –

did not detect a greater anxiety in girls than boys that would warrant more frequent discussion.

Table 20
"Why have your parents made a point of talking to you about the Gulf War?"

		Sex		Age	
	Total	Male	Female	9–12	13–15
Sample base	76	43	31	44	30
Reasons for parents talking about the Gulf War					
Ask if you are worried/afraid/tell not to worry	11 / 14%	4 / 9%	7 / 23%	7 / 16%	3 / 10%
Explain politics/history/background	9 / 12%	5 / 12%	4 / 13%	6 / 14%	3 / 10%
Talk about ecology/wildlife/environment	5 / 7%	4 / 9%	1 / 3%	2 / 5%	3 / 10%
Talk about weapons/equipment used	10 / 13%	10 / 23%	–	3 / 7%	5 / 17%
Discuss specific incident seen on television	5 / 7%	2 / 5%	3 / 10%	1 / 2%	4 / 13%
Discuss specific incident seen in newspaper	3 / 4%	–	3 / 10%	1 / 2%	2 / 7%
Discuss specific incident heard about on radio	1 / 1%	1 / 2%	–	–	1 / 3%
Explain war is right	4 / 5%	2 / 5%	2 / 6%	3 / 7%	1 / 3%
Explain war is wrong	7 / 9%	3 / 7%	3 / 10%	4 / 9%	2 / 7%
Talk about terrorism/threats in Britain/ say what they think will happen here	6 / 8%	1 / 2%	5 / 16%	3 / 7%	2 / 7%
Talk about family/friends involved in war/living or working in Middle East	9 / 12%	6 / 14%	3 / 10%	6 / 14%	3 / 10%
Say what they think will happen	13 / 17%	6 / 14%	6 / 19%	7 / 16%	5 / 17%

Base: All whose parents have made a point of talking about the Gulf War.

However, having offered that warning, it must also be borne in mind that when talking about anxiety there is no intention of using the term in any clinical sense of extreme agitation leading to neurotic or unusual behaviour that might readily be observed by a parent, but rather anxiety

45

of a low-key nature that results simply in manageable worry. Indeed, as we have seen in the manner in which the children discussed terrorism, the children did express anxiety, but not to the extent that it interfered with general psychological performance, or at least as far as could be detected by the accounts of their daily social interactions – they appeared little different during the war from before the war, and the concern about the IRA was a long-standing one. The biggest factor in minimizing worry was that Iraq was seen as a long way away: 'I suppose if Iraq was as close as France you would be more worried, but the bombs can't get to Britain'; and, 'It's different to the world wars because it's so far away, its not like Hitler being able to get over here.'

It must be noted in discussing anxiety or worry amongst children that only 39 per cent of the total sample made a point of asking their parents about the war and that only 36 per cent, according to the reports of the children, mentioned that their parents had made a point of talking to them about the war. Of the 36 per cent of parents who did make a point of talking about the war with their children, the main reason for doing so was to ask them if they were worried or afraid about the war and to tell them not to worry (14 per cent) (Table 20). Although the bases are small, it is nevertheless interesting since it fits with the general trend, that 23 per cent of girls had been approached by their parents to ask if they were worried, compared to only 9 per cent of boys. After talking about whether they were worried by the war, the next most common topic of conversation by parents with their children was that of weapons used (13 per cent). But no girl reported that their parents raised the topic of weapons and equipment with them. This score of 13 per cent was generated totally by the boys' responses. It is worth considering the possibility, therefore, that the manner in which the family regards boys and girls may well be responsible for the increased anxiety in girls when it comes to social and political issues such as war. In short, they are taught to worry. And this teaching, or transference of anxiety, is as likely as not based on assumptions that girls will be more bothered by such events without the realization that such a gender distinction has its own self-fulfilling prophecy.

However, whatever concern there was on the part of children about the war, it would not appear that this manifested itself in a great amount of family discussion. It may be that the British family is not given to 'talking through' problems or concerns and that, whatever worries the children had, they restricted council to their friends. Indeed, 71 per cent had talked with their friends about the war, but when the topics of conversation are examined the list of mentions does not indicate concern, but rather interest in events and happenings. Of the twenty-five subjects of conversation that children mentioned they had discussed with their friends, the top five mentioned were: weapons and equipment used (30 per cent), what might happen in the war (19 per cent), ecology/wildlife and environment (15 per cent), specific incidents seen on television (13 per cent), and whether war was right or wrong (11 per cent) (Table 21).

Table 21
"What exactly have you talked about with your friends?"

		Sex		Age	
	Total	Male	Female	9–12	13–15
Sample base	150	89	58	64	83
Worries/fears	15	7	7	6	8
	10%	8%	12%	9%	10%
Politics/history/background	9	4	5	3	4
	6%	4%	9%	5%	5%
Ecology/wildlife/environment	22	7	15	12	10
	15%	8%	26%	19%	12%
Weapons/equipment used	45	38	6	16	27
	30%	43%	10%	25%	33%
Discuss specific incident seen on television	19	8	10	5	14
	13%	9%	17%	8%	17%
Discuss specific incident seen in newspaper	6	2	4	–	6
	4%	2%	7%	–	7%
Discuss specific incident heard about on radio	2	2	–	–	2
	1%	2%	–	–	2%
Discuss whether war is right or wrong	17	10	7	7	9
	11%	11%	12%	11%	11%
Terrorism/threats in Britain/what will happen here	9	4	5	2	6
	6%	4%	9%	3%	7%
Family/friends involved in war/living or working in Middle East	17	7	10	10	7
	11%	8%	17%	16%	8%
Ask what they think will happen	29	13	15	16	12
	19%	15%	26%	25%	14%
Airmen held hostage in Iraq	3	1	2	1	2
	2%	1%	3%	2%	2%
Saddam evil/bad, etc.	14	9	5	4	10
	9%	10%	9%	6%	12%
Cost of war (money)	1	–	1	–	1
	1%	–	2%	–	1%
Deaths/injuries to Iraqi civilians	1	–	1	–	1
	1%	–	2%	–	1%

	Total	Sex		Age	
		Male	Female	9–12	13–15
Sample base	150	89	58	64	83
Deaths/injuries to Iraqi military	1	–	1	–	1
	1%	–	2%	–	1%
Deaths/injuries to Allied military	3	2	1	2	1
	2%	2%	2%	3%	1%
Playing war games	2	2	–	1	1
	1%	2%	–	2%	1%
Latest news (generally)	9	6	3	2	7
	6%	7%	5%	3%	8%
Who was winning/state of the war	12	8	4	8	4
	8%	9%	7%	13%	5%
Injuries/tortures/putting lives at risk	5	2	3	4	1
	3%	2%	5%	6%	1%
How brave the soldiers were	5	2	3	2	3
	3%	2%	5%	3%	4%
When Kuwait was invaded	1	–	1	–	1
	1%	–	2%	–	1%
American and British hostages	1	1	–	–	1
	1%	1%	–	–	1%
Others	1	–	1	–	1
	1%	–	2%	–	1%
Can't remember/don't know/not stated	3	1	2	1	2
	2%	1%	3%	2%	2%

Base: All who have talked to friends about the Gulf War.

Discussion with their friends about their worries and fears was the seventh highest mention, with 10 per cent saying that is what they had talked to their friends about. As with all such responses, the absolute percentage is not as important as the differences between the items scored. That is, it does not matter whether 30 per cent of children actually discussed military items or whether the true figure ought to have been 35 per cent; no more than that 19 per cent said they discussed what they thought might happen when the actual figure ought to have been 24 per cent. What the figures represent are differences in importance to them of the various topics discussed. And in this light it is noteworthy that worries or fears that the children had came seventh in the list of topics discussed. There is, however, a limit to any methodology, and the survey returns can tell us nothing about the intensity of the conversation, and mention of the flight range of a Scud missile or the fire power of an AK47 cannot be compared on some kind of numeric score with what it represents in terms of emotional involvement for the child as, say, a discussion of fear about the possibility of a 'terrorist' exploding a chemical weapon in their neighbourhood. Having said that, had children been suffering from anxiety, it could be expected that more mentions of discussion with friends about their concerns would have been scored. What is interesting is that when the scores are looked at more closely the conversation with friends appears to offer some support to the idea that what the children talked about was what they were actually interested in, and was not based on anxieties rooted in the war. For example, 43 per cent of the boys talked to their friends about weapons and equipment, compared to only 10 per cent of girls. The girls were much more likely to have talked with their friends about ecology/wildlife and the environment than were the boys – 26 per cent and 8 per cent respectively. Talk about weapons amongst the boys, and talk about the environment amongst the girls were, by far, the most common topics of conversation.

It may be that the girls' discussion of the environment had elements of anxiety attached to it, but looking at all the topics which children talked about with their friends, it looks very much as if the girls followed the war in a more 'adult' fashion. That is, their lack of interest in weaponry broadened their span of attention to other issues. For example, 26 per cent of girls talked with their friends about what they thought might happen in the war compared to 15 per cent of boys, and 17 per cent of girls discussed specific incidents seen on television compared to 9 per cent of boys. It is the wider attention that the girls paid to the war that might well account for the perceived higher levels of anxiety exhibited by the girls. That is, because the boys had an overriding interest in weaponry and in military hardware in general; this meant that the war took on the flavour of an adventure story more than it did for the girls. For the boys, and there was evidence of this in the group discussions, the war had an element of excitement to it that mitigated against the development of anxiety.

Although children were much more likely to talk with their friends than they were with their parents about specific points of the war, talk was not restricted to friends and family alone. Many of the children in the sample had classroom based discussions about the war with their teachers – the boys in the Northern group did confess that they would deliberately play on the teacher's known sensitivity about war and the possible worry it might be causing the children, by falsely initiating discussion as a way of wriggling out of formal lessons.

However, to the survey question, 'Have you had any classes at school which were about the Gulf War?' 35 per cent said that they had. The girls in the sample were more likely to have had such classes than the boys – 39 per cent and 32 per cent respectively. The main subject classes within which the war was discussed were: general studies/humanities (35 per cent), religious education (28 per cent), history (20 per cent), english (15 per cent) and geography (13 per cent). The main topics of discussion in the classes were: political background/history of middle east (39 per cent) ecology/wildlife/environment (17 per cent), whether war was right or wrong (16 per cent), and reassure children/tell them not to worry (15 per cent).

Whilst 35 per cent of children had specific classes on the Gulf War, 58 per cent had attended general school assemblies in which the war was introduced as a theme for address. Of the 58 per cent who had attended such assemblies, 27 per cent reported that the politics and background history of the Middle East had been explained. The next most common theme of the assemblies was reassurance of the children, telling them not to worry about the war (19 per cent). Of the 23 themes which the children mentioned as being raised in assembly, the only other two of any note were, ecology/wildlife/environment (13 per cent), and the Offering of prayers for everyone fighting in the Gulf (13 per cent).

Quite clearly the children in the sample had been exposed to a fair degree of discussion about the Gulf War, and level of interest in the war would appear to have been high, given that 67 per cent said that they had paid more attention than usual to the news on television during the period of the war. Interest in such an event would, however, appear to have been age and gender related; the younger children paid less attention to the news than the older children. For example, of those aged between nine and twelve years old, 61 per cent said they had paid more attention to the news, whilst 75 per cent of those aged between thirteen and fifteen said they had paid more attention to the news during the war. Only 57 per cent of girls said that they had paid more attention to the news compared to 78 per cent of the boys. This latter finding is not surprising once it is accepted that the boys, with their interest in weaponry and military equipment, tended to view the war more in terms of an adventure than did the girls. For the boys, the news had an air of excitement attached to it, and consequently they could be expected to pay greater attention to the course of events as portrayed on television than did the girls.

Yet, despite the fact that the boys paid greater attention to the news than they claimed they normally did, it was the girls who were more likely to include items that they had seen on the news in their conversations with their friends. For example, 17 per cent of girls said they had discussed specific incidents that they had seen on television with their friends, compared to 9 per cent of boys saying that they had discussed specific incidents with their friends. This finding is intriguing in the light of the fact that boys were more likely to talk about the war with their friends than were the girls in the sample, and also that 79 per cent of the boys said that they usually talked with their friends about things they saw or heard in the news, compared to 69 per cent of girls saying that they usually talked about the news with their friends.

What may have occurred is that the boys talked about the war in more general terms than did the girls, and certainly from the group discussions the boys demonstrated an impressive knowledge about the weapons used. That is, whilst the boys followed the news with greater interest than normal, they did so, to a greater extent than the girls, to collect information about technical matters. In this sense, the news offered the opportunity for the indulgence of a 'hobby' in a way not open to the girls. It was certainly the impression gained in the group discussions that knowledge of weaponry – which was a better plane, the performance of various missiles – operated in their discussions with school mates to facilitate status and demonstrate learning, in the way that knowledge about any topic close to the interest of boys might be used. Given that this was the case, it is not surprising that boys should talk about the war more than girls, but that girls talked about specific incidents in the news because, not having any general interest in military matters as such, their attention was drawn to particular incidents of the war which for them warranted discussion.

If the interpretation here is correct, then what the girls were engaged in was following the war as news and not the performance of war. Indeed, when the children were asked if there was a particular picture or event that they saw on television during the Gulf War that 'sticks in your mind', then of the 69 per cent who did retain a particular image, boys were more likely to nominate 'Scud/Iraqi missile attacks on Israeli/Patriot shooting down Scuds' than were the girls – 15 per cent and 7 per cent respectively (Table 22). However, despite the dramatic nature of such pictures, the image that made the greatest impact with children in the sense of a lasting image, was that of the pictures of allied airmen being paraded on television – 14 per cent said that was the picture that stuck in their mind, 12 per cent said Scud attacks, and 12 per cent the video pictures of guided bombs. However, damage to the environment scored highly as a feature that stuck in their minds when the separate items mentioned are taken together. For example, 5 per cent mentioned oil slicks at sea, 5 per cent dead sea birds and 8 per cent 'damage to the environment'. Only 6 per cent mentioned the pictures of the destruction of the Amiriya bunker/shelter as the pictures that stuck in their minds. It was damage to the environment, but in particular the plight of oil soaked birds, that upset the younger children and stayed with them as their main image of the war. What bothered them was what they considered was an injustice: 'People can retaliate. He's [Saddam] cruel to all nature. It's the birds. I don't think it's fair, they haven't done anything.' 'He kills everything, he's a murderer.'

Table 22
"What is it that sticks in your mind?"

		Sex		Age	
Sample base	Total 146	Male 86	Female 55	9–12 75	13–15 68
Scud/Iraqi missile attacks/attacks on Israel/Patriots shooting down scuds	18 12%	13 15%	4 7%	11 15%	6 9%
Damage to buildings	11 8%	6 7%	5 9%	4 5%	7 10%
Deaths/injuries/bodies of civilians	8 5%	3 3%	4 7%	6 8%	2 3%
Deaths/injuries/bodies of soldiers	5 3%	2 2%	3 5%	2 3%	3 4%
Allied airmen held by Iraqis	20 14%	13 15%	7 13%	9 12%	10 15%
Pictures from air attacks/video of guided bombs/attacks on Iraqi boats	17 12%	11 13%	6 11%	7 9%	10 15%
Pictures of first night of the air war/Baghdad when war started	6 4%	4 5%	2 4%	2 3%	3 4%
Technology/computers used by Allies	1 1%	1 1%	– –	– –	1 1%
Iraqi bunker/shelter bombing	9 6%	7 8%	2 4%	2 3%	7 10%
Iraqi prisoners of war/crying/kissing Allied soldiers	8 5%	6 7%	1 2%	6 8%	2 3%
Specific weapons used by Allies/Tomahawks/ Cobras/battleships/tanks/planes, etc.	11 8%	9 10%	2 4%	6 8%	5 7%
Oil wells on fire/smoke	6 4%	2 2%	4 7%	2 3%	4 6%
Oil slicks at sea	7 5%	7 8%	– –	4 5%	3 4%

	Sex			Age	
	Total	Male	Female	9–12	13–15
Sample base	146	86	55	75	68
Dead seabirds (specific mention only)	7	4	3	4	3
	5%	5%	5%	5%	4%
Damage to environment	12	5	6	7	5
	8%	6%	11%	9%	7%
All the carnage left when war ended	5	4	1	2	3
	3%	5%	2%	3%	4%
Animals being shot/suffering	2	–	2	1	1
	1%		4%	1%	1%
When Iraqis bombed American tent	2	1	1	1	1
	1%	1%	2%	1%	1%
Pictures of soldiers in the desert crying	4	–	4	2	2
	3%	–	7%	3%	3%
When the UK tank blew up	2	1	1	2	–
	1%	1%	2%	3%	–
Hostages shown on television	1	–	1	–	1
	1%	–	2%	–	1%
Others	4	2	2	2	2
	3%	2%	4%	3%	3%
Can't remember/don't know/not stated	6	2	3	6	–
	4%	2%	5%	8%	–

Base: All with picture or event seen on television during the Gulf War that sticks in the mind.

Of course, in accounting for any picture that might 'stick in the mind', the fact of frequency of a picture appearing must be taken into account, and pictures of damage to the environment and the Scud attacks were of a more rolling nature than the single attack on the Amiriya bunker/shelter. But clearly, the pictures of the pilots being paraded on Iraqi television was not a continuing story and must, therefore, have offered a powerful image; indeed, in the group discussions, particular mention was made by the children of having found the pictures of the pilots upsetting. The basis for the upset stemmed, as did seeing pictures of oil soaked birds and surrendering, weeping, Iraqi soldiers, from the feeling of helplessness. The pictures of dead soldiers did not upset the children to the extent that pictures of wounded soldiers did, and again the reason given was that they wished they could do something to help, whereas the dead were simply dead.

It is intriguing to consider whether the social action teaching in schools, along with television campaigns and popular music concerts, to raise awareness of world problems, may have helped foster a generation of children who are easily emotionally moved to accept individual responsibility, in terms of wishing to help, for any apparent tragedy. That is, they have been taught to be concerned about plight, be it the cutting down of rain forests, the effects of acid rain, the destruction of wildlife, or the ravages wrought by famine, which has engendered a social sensitivity towards images of suffering or devastation that leads to a willingness to want to help, even though the events witnessed are totally outside of their control to alter. In other words, the modern politics of aid or the modern politics of conservation, which utilize the mass media, television in particular, to generate not simply money but mass sympathy as a pressure for direct political action, has had the effect of stimulating the belief that the individual ought to act upon scenes of suffering or destruction. Children watching the ravages of war on television seem to respond similarly, and the manner in which the Amiriya bunker/shelter incident was reported in Britain, with eye witness accounts and statements from grieving relatives – was in some ways handled in the manner of a civil tragedy, such as an earthquake.

Table 23
"During the Gulf War were you worried or upset about anything you saw or heard?"

	Total	Sex		Age	
		Male	Female	9–12	13–15
Sample base	212	117	90	111	97
Very worried	19	8	10	8	10
	9%	7%	11%	7%	10%
Fairly worried	89	42	46	48	41
	42%	36%	51%	43%	42%
Not very worried	34	22	11	17	16
	16%	19%	12%	15%	16%
Not at all worried	67	45	20	37	28
	32%	38%	22%	33%	29%
Don't know/not stated	3	–	3	1	2
	1%	–	3%	1%	2%

Base: All children.

Whatever might be the changed consciousness of children as a result of social involvement broadcasting, what is not in doubt is the fact that television provided more focus for topics of discussion about the war amongst children than did any other media. For example, when all those who said that they had talked with their friends about the war were asked 'What exactly have you talked about with your friends?', 13 per cent mentioned that they had discussed specific incidents seen on television, 4 per cent items they had read in newspapers, and 1 per cent incidents heard on radio.

We do not know the substance of the discussion about the incidents seen on television, but 51 per cent of the total sample said that they had been either worried or upset by things that they saw or heard during the Gulf War. However, only 9 per cent of the 51 per cent said that they had been very worried or upset (Table 23). No differences in levels of worry emerged between the two age bands of 9–12 and 13–15, but differences did emerge between the boys and the girls – 62 per cent of the girls said that they had been worried or upset compared to 43 per cent of the boys.

In terms of items that had caused worry or upset, the top three were: allied pilots/hostages beaten up (18 per cent), oil wells set alight/oil spills/wildlife at risk/dead sea-birds (18 per cent), and death/killing/suffering (17 per cent) (Table 24). The next highest mention at 12 per cent was 'worried about war coming here/that it would last a long time'. What is interesting from the top three scores is that marked differences occurred between the sexes over what worried or upset them – 28 per cent of the boys said that they were worried/upset by the allied pilots/hostages, compared to only 9 per cent of the girls. The evidence gained in the group discussions is that the boys had been affected by the pictures of the shot down pilots shown as captives on Iraqi television more than the girls, but in a very aggressive, militaristic way. Their response was one of anger that prisoners of war should be treated in such a manner and led to denunciations of Saddam Hussein and, in one or two instances, comments that the war should have been pushed on with even greater vigour. The girls on the other hand were more likely to have been worried/upset by instances of death/killing/suffering than were the boys – 21 per cent and 12 per cent respectively.

This difference may well be accounted for in part by the fact that, as mentioned, the girls in the sample were less certain than the boys that it was right for Britain to join the other nations in war with Iraq, and therefore were more exposed to feelings of senselessness, and consequently upset, at the death and suffering that the war brought. It could be, of course, but we have no ways of knowing from this study, that differences in children exist between the sexes towards the portrayal of suffering, but if that is the case, then, judging by the responses in the adult group discussions, which were deliberately designed through the use of film to detect attitudes to the portrayal of death and injury, such differences are not present in later years: the women showed no greater sensitivity to death and injury than the men.

The frequency of being upset or worried by incidents relating to the risk to wildlife/oil wells set alight/oil spillage/dead sea-birds, was exactly the same between the sexes, but differences in responses emerged in terms of worry about war coming to Britain or that the war would last a long time. Although only 12 per cent of the total sample – the fourth highest score – expressed such concern, 18 per cent of those that did were girls, compared to 6 per cent of those who were boys. This finding is not difficult to explain.

Table 24
"What was it in particular that worried or upset you?"

	Sex			Age	
Sample base	Total 108	Male 50	Female 56	9–12 56	13–15 51
Worried about possibility of friends/relatives being hurt/captured/at risk, etc.	11 10%	3 6%	7 13%	5 9%	6 12%
Allied pilots/hostages beaten up	19 18%	14 28%	5 9%	8 14%	11 22%
Oil wells set alight/oil spills/wildlife at risk/dead seabirds	19 18%	9 18%	10 18%	8 14%	11 22%
Chemical/germ/biological weapons	3 3%	2 4%	1 2%	2 4%	1 2%
Bombing of Iraq (unspecified)	3 3%	2 4%	1 2%	– –	3 6%
Bombing of Iraq (civilians/houses)	3 3%	1 2%	2 4%	2 4%	1 2%
Felt sorry for Iraqis/forced to fight/not their fault	4 4%	2 4%	1 2%	3 5%	1 2%
Saddam Hussein's actions/character	5 5%	1 2%	4 7%	4 7%	1 2%
Upset by dead/wounded/relatives of dead/wounded seen/heard/read about	8 7%	3 6%	5 9%	3 5%	5 10%
Land war phase of Gulf War	1 1%	– –	1 2%	1 2%	– –
British casualties resulting from American attacks/'friendly fire'	2 2%	1 2%	1 2%	– –	2 4%
Didn't understand what was going on/why it happened	1 1%	1 2%	– –	1 2%	– –
Death/killing/suffering	18 17%	6 12%	12 21%	6 11%	12 24%

	Sex			Age	
Sample base	Total 108	Male 50	Female 56	9–12 56	13–15 51
Fear for self being involved/called up to war	3 3%	3 6%	– –	2 4%	1 2%
Worried about war coming here/that it would last a long time	13 12%	3 6%	10 18%	8 14%	5 10%
Innocent people being injured/killed	11 10%	5 10%	6 11%	6 11%	5 10%
Fighting/bombing (unspecified)	3 3%	2 4%	1 2%	3 5%	– –
British and American forces	2 2%	2 4%	– –	1 2%	1 2%
Retreat from Kuwait by Iraqis	2 2%	1 2%	1 2%	1 2%	1 2%
Bombing of bunker	2 2%	2 4%	– –	– –	2 4%
Others	2 2%	2 4%	– –	1 2%	– –
Can't remember/don't know/not stated	3 3%	2 4%	1 2%	2 4%	1 2%

Base: All who were worried or upset by anything during the Gulf War.

There is evidence from the survey that the girls had less interest in the weaponry of war than did the boys, but what was particularly obvious in the group discussions was that not only did the girls have little interest in matters military, but that they possessed scant knowledge of the capability of weapons. Hence, it was the girls, more than the boys, who thought Iraq might possess the military capability of targeting Britain direct. It is not surprising, therefore, that they should express greater concern that the war might engulf their homeland since, as far as they were concerned, that was a possibility. It was a quite rational fear. However, this worry was not one they lived with for very long since, as the girls in the group discussions mentioned, they fairly quickly came to realize that Iraq did not possess long range weapons capable of inflicting damage on Britain. In other words, as more knowledge was acquired, anxiety lessened.

The children were not asked to state the sources of their knowledge about the war, but they were asked direct questions about the reports that they saw or heard during the war. Most children said that they thought the reports that came from journalists in Iraq were censored –

67 per cent thought they were censored; only 11 per cent thought they were not censored, but 22 per cent did not know (Table 25). Of those that did believe the reports were censored, 55 per cent considered that the Iraqi government had been the agent of censorship, and 20 per cent the Iraqi military. Only 4 per cent considered that the British government had censored the reports from Iraq. Belief that reports were censored rose with age – 59 per cent of those aged 9–11 considered censorship had occurred, compared to 77 per cent of 13–15 year olds. Amongst the adult population, 93 per cent considered that reports from Iraq had been censored. When children were asked if they thought the reports from journalists with 'our forces' were censored, 42 per cent thought that they were – 34 per cent thought they were not and 24 per cent did not know (Table 26).

Table 25
"Do you think the reports which came from journalists in Iraq were censored at all?"

		Sex		Age	
	Total	Male	Female	9–12	13–15
Sample base	212	117	90	111	97
Yes	143	84	57	65	75
	67%	72%	63%	59%	77%
No	23	15	7	15	8
	11%	13%	8%	14%	8%
Don't know/not stated	46	18	26	31	14
	22%	15%	29%	28%	14%

Base: All children.

Table 26
"Do you think the reports from journalists who were actually with our forces were censored?"

		Sex		Age	
	Total	Male	Female	9–12	13–15
Sample base	212	117	90	111	97
Yes	90	51	38	44	44
	42%	44%	42%	40%	45%
No	72	43	27	34	37
	34%	37%	30%	31%	38%
Don't know/not stated	50	23	25	33	16
	24%	20%	28%	30%	16%

Base: All children.

What is interesting is that the gap between the older and younger children practically closes, which might suggest that although the older children had a more highly developed grasp of the realities of war reporting, it did not extend to understanding the part that information is held to play by government and military in relaying events to its own civilian population. However, the adult survey showed a drop in the number of people who considered that reports from the coalition forces were censored, when compared with beliefs about reports from Iraq being censored – 76 per cent thought the reports from the coalition were censored.

Because a report is censored does not of courses mean that it is untrue, and the children were asked, 'Did you hear any news stories on television about the Gulf War which you did not think were entirely true?', to which 27 per cent said 'yes'. Again the older children were much more likely not to have believed reports (33 per cent) than the younger children (23 per cent). It is difficult to compare the adult responses in the area of trusting reports with those of the children, since adults were asked more questions of a complicated nature. But only 20 per cent said that they trusted the news 'a lot' that came from journalists in Baghdad, whereas 41 per cent trusted the news 'a lot' that came from journalists with the coalition forces. Quite clearly, the adult viewer was much more likely to be suspicious of news from within the enemy sphere of influence, but judging from the children's answers to the question, 'Which one television news story did you think was the most difficult to believe?' then, from those who said they did not believe all they saw or heard, by far the largest category of distrust was reserved for 'any Iraq claims' (23 per cent). Of the seventeen coded answers, the next highest nomination was also based on disbelief in Iraqi truthfulness – 9 per cent cited Iraqi claims about the number of allied aircraft shot down. And in the group discussions it was quite clear that the children brought a distinct critical faculty into play when viewing Iraqi shot pictures: 'Saddam Hussein shows all those pictures of people shaking his hand, but you don't believe it, it's not true, because he's just making it up to think that people like Saddam Hussein, but they don't.'

It would seem that, for both adults and children, Iraq lost the propaganda war on the simple grounds that it was not trusted as a source of information. However, it might be expected that reports that were seen to be under the restriction of enemy authorities would not be accorded the same level of trust as that given to reports that were seen to be under the restrictions of friendly authorities, but it is interesting that the children in our sample did not always believe that which they saw or heard from the allied side. The fact that scepticism grew with age indicates that information, even in children, is sifted against their existing understanding of how the world operates and against their own canons for establishing truth. That is, the older children who were in possession of more information about the war, and in possession of greater understanding about human behaviour, were less likely to take things on trust than the younger children. In some ways, the way the children handled information was not dissimilar to the way in which they handled their own anxieties about the war – they tested, no matter how sophisticatedly, their fears and understandings against given information, and then circulated that information in social contact with others to arrive at a manageable operating position.

In so far as seeing images of destruction is concerned, then the children did appear to be protected to a certain extent by the same type of thinking that characterized the adult responses; namely, that the war was considered to be just and that the misfortunes of the Iraqi people were nobody's fault but their leader's:

> Well, if he's [Saddam] going to invade another country it serves him right that people are going to like bomb his electricity supplies and everything. They're always showing all these pictures of you know Iraqis going out to collect water and it's not fair because even though we see them, yes, but it's his fault, he's forcing that on his people because he invaded Kuwait.

But, in so far as images of injury are concerned, it is difficult to say that such feelings of justice and placement of blame for the suffering on Saddam did protect the children to the same extent as it did the adults. One major difference, perhaps, is that the children did not operate with a firm historical understanding of war and what war involves, in the way that their parents did. There was from the children, for example, no fatalistic statements to the effect that death and injury are just part of war and must be expected and accepted as part of the policy of waging war.

The children were asked if they had seen pictures of the destruction of the Amiriya bunker/shelter (they were not shown the newsreels) on television, and many had. Asked what they thought when they saw them, they did say they found them upsetting. 'I found them upsetting really' said one young girl. And another girl said:

> It didn't look much at first you know because there was no bodies or anything, it was all just rubble so there wasn't much really to see, but as it got further on into the interview, well not the interview, the reports, it got a lot more gory.

60

Asked how she felt about the gory pictures, she replied, 'I started to feel sorry for them when you saw the white sheets covering up the bodies and there were feet sticking out of the end.' But then another girl in the group offered the type of justification for the strike which the adults offered:

> But the Americans were right to bomb because they could have – if it was a military thing, I mean a communications thing like it seemed to be, then they'd have got our troops and it would have been even worse for our country wouldn't it?

It is doubtful that this type of justification afforded the same level of emotional protection from being upset by scenes of death and injury that it appeared to do for the adult viewers. As one young girl said: 'I think children get more upset than adults really', and then continued by saying 'I'd just put the gory ones on at night, and if people didn't want to watch them they didn't have to.' Yet, others in the same group considered that the policy that existed was correct:

> I'd show the bunker because children need to know what happened, because if they don't know that's even worse, they're more scared if they don't know – if you just said what happened to the children some wouldn't understand it, you need pictures to be able to understand what happened.

Another said she wanted the truth because 'you don't want any little lie put around on television because that would make you more scared when you find out it's a lie.'

This insistence on honesty, which they clearly thought pictures provided in a way that words alone could not, is not surprising, since what frightened the children, as we have seen from their earlier statements, is not so much the brutal scenes of war, but uncertainty about the implications of what they were witnessing, and uncertainty about what it might mean for them in terms of their own existence and the existence of their families. Once they had the information to understand the course of events they were witnessing, anxiety was reduced. The simple lesson for television, and indeed for parents, is that rather than shelter children from the harsh events of the world, it is best to open those events to children in a manner in which they can understand what is taking place, and that includes scenes and images that might be considered upsetting. Of course, the scenes of the destruction of the bunker were upsetting for children, but then so they were for adults. What would seem to be more worry making for children is for them to be aware that something awful has taken place but not be able to visualize what that awfulness actually involved by being denied access to pictures of the event.

CONCLUSION

What the survey and the group discussions demonstrated is that the fear manifested in Britain – with reports in the press quoting school teachers, parents and others in close contact with children – that the coverage of the war generated high levels of anxiety in children, had little basis as a reality of children's lives. To begin with, as the survey shows, most children did not show high levels of anxiety on the indices taken, and in the group discussions it was obvious that any anxiety that had been created was not long lasting. Basically, the children handled anxiety in the same way that adults handle anxiety: they examined the grounds upon which, in part, the anxiety was based, and part of that base was uncertainty about how events would unfold and how they would affect them. Once information was gathered that gave greater certainty to proceedings and increased understanding of the likely effects of events on them and their families, anxiety was reduced. But also, children are not free-floating beings crashing against the news without the protection of stable social interactions. They talked to their parents, to some extent, about the war and their parents, to some extent, talked to them; but most of all they talked to their friends about the war. And, in terms of limiting anxiety with respect to events in the Gulf, they talked to their friends at school, but not about the war. The main topics of conversation at school, according to the children in the group discussions, were those topics that they always talked about – pop stars, sport, fashion and the other sex. The news and images transmitted from the Gulf had a difficult time finding space in the life of children whose time was taken up with the everyday existence of being a child.

3. Content

THE VISION AND VOICE OF THE WAR: THE CONTENT OF TELEVISION

So far we have examined the viewers' reactions, both adults and children, to the events in the Gulf, along with their attitudes towards issues such as censorship, and the portrayal of death and injury on television. Yet any study of the viewer's response to the Gulf War would be incomplete without an examination of the pictures and words that were broadcast to the viewer. Without knowing what the viewers saw and heard it is difficult to account for the attitudes which the viewers formed about the war. Of course, the pictures seen and the words spoken during the Gulf War did not shape the attitudes displayed in any total sense: attitudes are formed through a complex interplay of values and understandings of the social world and information received. A racist, for example, will 'receive' news about an event in the black townships of South Africa which is different from that of a liberal. And so with news from the Gulf. It could be expected that a pacifist would give different responses to a question about the portrayal of injury sustained in war, as an arch-militarist – or, if the responses were the same, the reasoning underpinning the responses is likely to be so different as to make the two responses in effect different. Questionnaire surveys cannot always capture the reasoning behind the responses which might make the ostensibly same responses different. Hence the use of group discussions to add insight into what might be at work in the viewers' responses to our survey questions.

Given that it is difficult to 'get at' the understandings that people have towards issues and events even by direct questioning or interrogation, it would be wrong to move from an examination of the content of television to crude mechanistic assumptions about the part such content plays, or the effect that it has, on the attitudes and views of those watching the news. However, it would also be wrong to ignore content altogether in mapping attitudes to the war, as if somehow it played no part in shaping the views that people held. When people answered our questions about the Gulf, in both the survey and the group discussions, their answers were based on something, and part of that something is what they had seen and heard in the news. Indeed, as we have seen from the group discussions, support for the positions that people gave was 'evidenced' by reference to what they had seen and heard on television.

The content analysis, of which the presented findings are merely preliminary to the full findings once the huge amount of data is finally coded and analysed, is based upon nearly three hundred miles of tape recordings of the news begun slightly prior to the war and for the duration of the war. The sample taken ran from 14/01/91 (three days before the Coalition attack began) to 3/03/91 (when the ceasefire was agreed) and included the main evening news programmes broadcast on six channels.

The programmes were:

BBC1	–	*The Nine O'clock News* normally at 21.00 hours
BBC2	–	*Newsnight* normally at 22.30 hours
ITV	–	*The News at Ten* normally at 22.00 hours
C4	–	*The Channel 4 News* normally at 19.00 hours
Sky	–	*Sky World News* normally at 23.00 hours to 23.30 hours
CNN	–	Output on the News Channel normally at 21.00 hours to 22.00 hours (UK time)

Each programme was divided into discrete units each of which reported on a particular news story. These units are called *items*. The analysis of items provided information on the basic content of news stories which focused on the Gulf War (the people involved, the subject or 'event' discussed, the type of pictures shown, reporting restrictions etc.). For greater depth of analysis, eight areas of interest were then selected by the research team and examined in detail. These areas of interest are called *aspects* and were coded in order to provide details of the portrayal of military activities and their results in terms of human death or injury, political relations, societies and people affected by the war, peace negotiations, the way human rights were reported, economic relations and, finally, damage to the environment.

More than one aspect of the Gulf War could be coded for any one item.

For example, if the news item which reported on a Scud attack on Israel also included pictures of dead or injured people both the military and violence aspects of the report would be coded. If a report on a Scud attack on Israel also included information on the ways in which Israeli people were preparing for these attacks both the military and social aspects of the report would be coded.

FINDINGS

During the sample period, a total of 3713 separate news items were counted in 274 programmes over 183 hours. Nearly three quarters (71 per cent) of these items reported on news from the Gulf, totalling 143 hours of television. Thus, non-Gulf items accounted for only 40 hours or 22 per cent of news broadcast time and constituted only 29 per cent of the total news items shown during the sample period (Table 27). Moreover, items on the Gulf were on average one third longer than the non-Gulf items (3 and 2 minutes respectively). It is perhaps not surprising, then, that of those viewers who were dissatisfied with the coverage of the war, one of their main objections was that it was given too much coverage (see Table 2 of the audience section). However, it must be pointed out that those who were dissatisfied with coverage given by television represented only 12 per cent of the total sample and it is more than likely, therefore, that the 38 per cent of those who gave as the reason for their dissatisfaction that television 'devoted too much space' to the war were not that interested in following the war, although in the group discussions a feeling did emerge from viewers whilst not being dissatisfied with the coverage to any great extent, that the war was 'overplayed'.

Table 27. Frequency of number and length of Gulf and non-Gulf items: channel comparisons

	BBC1	BBC2	ITV	C4	Sky	CNN	Total
No. of items on Gulf	635	369	352	322	344	599	2621
No. of items on non-Gulf	188	42	159	276	152	275	1092
Total number of items	82.3	411	511	598	496	874	3713
Total coverage – Gulf (hours)	24.0	30.1	21.0	23.9	13.4	30.9	143.3
Total coverage – non-Gulf (hours)	5.2	4.9	5.7	11.1	6.0	7.1	40.0
Total coverage (hours)	29.2	35.0	26.7	35.0	19.4	38.0	183.3
% of total broadcast time devoted to Gulf	82	86	79	68	69	81	78
Average length of items on Gulf (mins)	2.3	4.9	3.6	4.5	2.3	3.1	3.3
Average length of items non-Gulf (mins)	1.7	7.0	2.2	2.4	2.4	1.6	2.2
Number of programmes	49	40	49	44	43	49	274

It is not surprising, given the nature of the event, that Gulf News should fill the screens and push out other stories. Had the war gone on longer, then it is likely that other stories would have, at least at times, pushed the war away from the 'front page'. The number of stories that managed to achieve this feat during the Gulf War was very small indeed. Non-Gulf war made the headlines in only 15 per cent of cases, and featured as the lead story in only 5 per cent of cases. Examples include the IRA attack on Downing Street (7/2/91), the cold weather and storms across the UK (9/2/91) and the budget in the USA. Non-Gulf news which was relatively frequently reported in the headlines, but which was not used as the lead story, included reports on political tension in Lithuania, the trial of Winnie Mandela and domestic fears over the National Health Service in the UK.

Given the heavy financial investment that television news services committed to the Gulf, and the obvious public interest through direct involvement of British forces in the war, it is hardly surprising that the Gulf news captured the centre stage of affairs. Yet there is no doubt that the development of events in the Baltic States which had very long term implications for the structure of European and even world affairs, were not given the prominence that they perhaps deserved. Thus, whilst it would be wrong to criticize television for focusing its coverage on events in the Gulf, the level of concentration might be criticized when it is considered that the major complaint made by the viewer was the repetitive nature of the coverage (see Table 2). This criticism was also raised in the group discussions.

Turning to the coverage of the war itself, Table 28a shows the frequency counts for Gulf-related news items. In the sample taken, a total of 143 hours of evening news coverage focused on the Gulf War. During this time 2621 separate items were counted covering 3954 war events. Events were used to locate an item to a specific occasion during the war (such as a Scud attack or the Battle of Khafji), a general activity (e.g. religious activity, coalition air attack) or state of affairs (for example the effect of war on the economy or international relations) or a particular area of concern (such as racism, P.o.W's, Saddam Hussein, censorship). Up to 3 events could be coded per item in order to reference them. What we notice from Table 28a is that general war progress and speculation about the threat of a ground war dominated the news items, followed by reports concerned with coalition air attacks and Scud attacks. The 'event', 'general war progress', was used to code any item which concerned itself with a whole range of general war activities such as troop movements, attack strategies, weaponry development etc. (such as 'speculation grows that a ground offensive could come sooner rather than later', Sky, 13/02/91).

Table 28a. Frequency of events record in Gulf items

Type of event	Occur-rences N	%	Type of event	Occur-rences N	%
General war progress	332	8	Liberation of Kuwait City	27	1
Threat of Ground War	267	7	Use of patriot missiles	26	1
Allied air attack	212	5	Media coverage	24	1
SCUD attack	202	5	Censorship	21	1
Non-specified peace initiative	190	5	Iraqi defection of troops	21	1
International political relations	167	4	Future of Middle East	21	1
Military preparations for war	134	3	Press conferences	21	1
Future progress of war	111	3	Anti-west demonstrations	19	1
Prisoners of war	100	3	SCUD launchers	18	1
Present state of affairs in Iraq	95	2	Refugees fleeing Iraq	18	1
Political preparation for war	95	2	UN deadline of Iraqi withdrawal	18	1
Military aircraft losses	76	2	Initial start of hostilities	17	-
Present state of affairs in Kuwait	75	2	Racism and minorities	17	-
Threat of Israeli retaliation	71	2	Failure of French peace initiative	14	-
Saddam Hussein (general)	69	2	Peace initiative France	13	-
Oil slick	66	2	Failure of De Cuellar peace initiative	12	-
International repercussions of war	66	2	De Cuellar peace initiative	12	-
Civilian loss of life	66	2	Order to withdraw to Iraq troops	12	-
Effects of war on US society	64	2	Human shield	12	-
Bombing of Baghdad	56	1	Liberation of Kuwait Island	12	-
Kuwaiti oil fields on fire	55	1	Pro-war civilian demonstration	10	-
Military personnel losses	55	1	EEC role in peace initiatives	9	-
Terrorist attacks	51	1	Deadlines expire	9	-
Israeli role in war	50	1	Military land losses	9	-
Iraqi planes to Iran	49	1	Military naval losses	9	-
Future of Iraq	46	1	History of Kuwait/Iraq	8	-
Civilian peace demonstration	44	1	Sanctions	8	-
Iraqi claims	44	1	Initial invasion of Kuwait 2/8/90	8	-
Military briefing	43	1	Royal/Presidential visits	8	-
Effect of war on UK society	42	1	Pro-Saddam demonstration	8	-
Allied naval attack	40	1	Psychological effects of war on people	6	-
Effects of economy	39	1	Disputes over oil fields	6	-
Iranian peace initiative	39	1	Psychological effects of war on troops	5	-
Baghdad bunker	39	1	Saddam Hussein with troops	5	-
Saddam's conditional peace offer	39	1	Use of decoys	5	-
Reference to previous wars	37	1	Religious ceremonies	3	-
National address by leader	36	1	US society pre-war	3	-
Social preparations for war	32	1	Support lines	1	-
Meetings/negotiations	31	1	Iraqi supergun	1	-
Parliamentary debates	31	1	History of UN	1	-
Financial aid	29	1	Other non-specified Gulf events	66	2
UK/US detainees, deportations	28	1			
			TOTAL	**3954**	**99**

Because of the very nature of war, it is not surprising that the highest frequency of coverage should be given to the general movement of troops, war materials and the action of battle. But what is interesting is that the importance of the event itself – war – appears to swamp the news and did so at the expense of discussion about either the initial invasion of Kuwait in August 1990, or the presentation of a historical perspective on the war. Of course, it can be argued that the role of news is to cover events as they occur and not relate those events into some kind of overall framework of meaning. But if that is the case, and despite the role of current affairs in countering the news as history fractured and frozen in the present, there was evidence in the groups that the viewer, outside of the immediate reason for war, had little grasp of the wider political situation and relationships by which to make sense of the events which the news carried.

History is made by individuals that act, but if those acts are stripped of any context within which the acts occur, understanding of why something happened is left at the level of the individual and explanation over-focusses on the personality of the actor. It is not surprising, therefore, as we saw from the comments made in the group discussion, that Saddam Hussein was viewed as mad. Not armed with any general understanding of the political and historical situation relating to the Gulf War, the only sense to be made of Saddam's actions was to deny that he had any sense. We will see later on in the content analysis how Saddam Hussein was portrayed.

It is difficult, within the existing conventions of news, to see how the news could be structured differently, and, as mentioned, it is the role of current affairs to flesh out understanding by providing in-depth analysis of the events reported in the news. But, and even accepting that viewing of current affairs rose during the Gulf war, generally not much more than 50 per cent of people view such programmes on a regular basis, compared to about 70–80 per cent of the population who watch the news on a regular basis. The point to make, therefore, is not so much a criticism of the news, but to offer an understanding of how the viewer comes to his or her understanding of the world, which then offers itself in the types of comments made in the course of the audience research part of the study.

If the presentation of war by television is one of arms and armaments rather than a presentation of the situation within which arms are used, it is also the case that it is presented as a male affair and of male concern. For example, when coding each item, a note was made of people who presented coverage of the Gulf War and those who were interviewed about it. In all 1525 separate appearances were coded. Of these 87 per cent were male and only 13 per cent were female. These were categorized according to three status categories – major presenters, minor presenters and interviewees. Major presenters were primarily located in the news studio where they introduced items and provided continuity throughout the news bulletin. Women enjoyed a relatively high proportional representation as major presenters, contributing 22 per cent of such appearances (see Table 28b).

Minor presenters were generally located outside the studio where their primary role was to contribute information to specific items through reports. Where journalists were interviewed about their situation, either by satellite links, or telephone, or in the studio, they were still coded as minor presenters. In comparison to major presenters women had proportionately less representation as minor presenters – only 13 per cent of all minor presenters were women.

Interviewees were coded either by specific names (as in the case of Saddam Hussein), professional or social groupings (e.g. politicians, doctor/medical personnel) or by their contribution to the item in terms of specialist knowledge (e.g. military expert) or experience (e.g. victim, refugee). Women were poorly represented in this status category – they constituted only 8 per cent of all people interviewed in Gulf items.

Table 28b. Frequency of major presenters, minor presenters and interviewees in Gulf items

Major presenter	N	%
Martyn Lewis	347	12
Jon Snow	277	10
Michael Buerk	249	9
Nikki Marx	148	5
Scott Chisholm	146	5
Julia Somerville	142	5
Cheryl Atkinson	141	5
Trevor McDonald	134	5
Peter Snow	118	4
Lou Waters	96	3
Ralph Wenge	78	3
Alastair Burnet	68	2
Alastair Stewart	65	2
Chris Mann	53	2
David Michael	51	2
Other major presenters	787	27
Total no. of appearances of all major presenters	2900	101

Minor presenter	N	%
Non-specified journalist at military briefing	192	9
Non-specified journalist at press conference	132	6
Mark Urban	46	2
Brent Sadler	45	2
David Shukman	41	2
Gavin Esler	40	2
Nik Gowing	40	2
Brian Barron	39	2
Brian Hanrahan	38	2
Bill Dunlop	34	2
Edward Stourton	35	2
Martin Bell	32	1
David Smith	31	1
Al Hinman	30	1
Martin Brunt	29	1
Other minor presenters	1412	64
Total no. of appearances of all minor presenters	2216	101

Interviewee	N	%
Unspecified armed forces personnel	584	11
Person in the street	439	8
Government politician or equivalent	328	6
Middle ranking officer	272	5
Diplomat or Ambassador	226	4
High ranking officer	194	4
Foreign Secretary	194	4
Non-specified political expert	150	3
Defence Secretary	148	3
George Bush	141	3
Military spokesperson	138	3
Opposition politician or equivalent	137	3
Military academic	95	2
Non-specified academic	93	2
John Major	93	2
Other interviewees	2156	40
Total no. of appearances of all interviewees	5388	99

Why the presentation of war is such a male event is not difficult to understand, but the actual proportions of male and female appearances, particularly with regard to interviewees, is fairly stark and more difficult to understand. What it means is that the coverage of war (and we can see this by referring back to Table 28a) was fairly tightly restricted to military matters, and did not move to include social issues, such as psychological effects of war on people or general concern about the war, which in turn might have allowed greater inclusion of women in the coverage.

Alongside the details of 'who' was telling 'what' about the war, the type of visual images[1] or pictures associated with the reports was also noted. Coding categories ranged from the general visuals of studios, graphics, minor presenters talking to camera etc., to more specific pictures: for example, injured or dead bodies, military equipment, prisoners of war and so on. The emphasis here was on capturing the overall visual nature of items rather than coding all specific visual images (which would have been too time consuming at this stage of the research). Thus, where an item included, for example, a studio shot followed by footage of pre-war Kuwait, followed by another studio shot followed by pictures of general wreckage, 'studio' would be coded once only, but pre-war Kuwait and general wreckage would each be coded separately.

Table 28c shows the full breakdown of the appearances of each type of visual image of picture content. In all 8028 images were observed. Over one half (54 per cent) were based in studios, showed interviews, reporters talking to camera and in still photographs, graphics and maps. Of the types of images associated with war activities, military press conferences were the most frequently portrayed (7 per cent of visual images coded, followed by footage of military equipment or manoeuvres (5 per cent). Injured or dead bodies, prisoners of war, refugees, civilian demonstrations (both for peace and pro-war) were rarely found (less than 1 per cent of visual images in each case).

It is interesting, when we look at Table 28c, that the amount of items that were studio-based was just over half. Thus, although this was the first real satellite war and helped foster, through the immediacy of pictures, the impression of being present as history was made, much of the news that was presented actually took place in the studio. Indeed, as noted earlier, only the Scud attacks were actually live. Furthermore, most of the pictures that were not studio based were of military press con-

---

1   *Image refers to a discrete visual image within the different types of picture content. These were coded by type of picture seen rather than frequencies. For example, if in a news item three different pictures of Tornados were seen in one continuous sequence 'military equipment manoeuvres' would be coded only once along with any other different types of pictures on the item (such as studio shot, or damage to city/town).*

ferences. Hardly the action of battle. Indeed, the fact that the most common visual image shown from outside the studio was that of military press conferences, provides a very clear picture of the news management of the war: press conferences, no matter what questioning of officials takes place, are a good example of the military running the news; that is, controlling the flow of information and setting the agenda for discussion by the selective release of information.

Table 28c. Picture content of Gulf War news items

Type of picture content	Incidents N	%
Studio	2257	28
Outside reporter talking to camera	561	7
Press conference	530	7
Outside formal interview	487	6
Military equipment manoeuvres	380	5
Civilian life	360	5
Military life	297	4
Graphics	278	4
Studio discussions	245	3
Non-expert interview	237	3
Meetings	237	3
Damage to cities/towns	227	3
Maps	213	3
Air attack (inc. pilots view)	179	2
Parliamentary debate	132	2
Land attack	124	2
Briefings (non military)	109	1
Still photograph (not reporter or military)	100	1
Military briefing	76	1
Damage to the environment	66	1
Civilian demonstration for peace	64	1
Military equipment capabilities	62	1
General wreckage	62	1
Damage to military equipment	54	1
Civilian demonstration, anti-West	53	1
Injured/dead bodies	51	1
Still pictures of reporters	49	1
Prisoners of war	45	1
Hospitalized injured/dead bodies	44	1
National address	42	1
Still photograph of Military equipment	40	1
Leaders residences	37	1
Military parade/show of weapons	36	–
Sea attack	35	–

Type of picture content	Incidents N	%
Saddam Hussein with people	34	–
Saddam Hussein with troops	34	–
Civilian demonstration pro-war	33	–
Footage of previous wars	32	–
Religious ceremonies	31	–
Hospitals	21	–
Refugees	18	–
Damage to oil wells	14	–
Royal/Presidential visit	14	–
Civilian preparations of war	10	–
Previous era footage	8	–
Pre-war Kuwait	5	–
Public debates	3	–
Stock exchange	1	–
Support group meetings	1	–
TOTAL	8028	103

Very few pictures, as Table 28c shows, were of actual fighting – the stuff of war as most viewers would believe war to be. In fact, although not included in this formal content analysis, an examination of the news during the sample period showed that the most pictures of dramatic action broadcast were from fighting that took place in the Baltics, not the Gulf. Admittedly, the conflict in the Baltics was of a different nature than that which occurred in the Gulf, and the fighting of a different order. The shooting of action footage was easier in the Baltics. But even allowing for the absence of clear 'fronts' in the Baltics, and the street fighting that took place when compared to the set piece battles and air attacks of the Gulf War, what cannot be overlooked in accounting for 'action' pictures in one case and the absence of action pictures in the other, is the difference in the reporting restrictions on journalists. In the case of the Baltics, there was no restriction on reporting. The journalists were allowed to manage as best they could, which meant that they achieved dramatic footage; whereas the tight control of reporting in the Gulf meant, notwithstanding the differences in the types of war, very few pictures of fighting, or indeed, of dead or injured. As Table 28c shows, only 1 per cent of visual images were of death and injury.

We have already dealt, in the Audience section of the study, with the viewers' attitudes towards censorship and will not, therefore, deal with it again here, except to note that the viewers' acceptance of restrictions on reporting only extended to information that might endanger coalition soldiers' lives. It did not extend to wishing for blanket control over the images of war. It is true, however, that they did not wish for a heavy diet of harrowing footage but, as we see from Table 28c, the absence of scenes of death and injury did not make this a particularly special issue during the Gulf War. What they did see, namely the carnage of the Amiriya bunker/shelter within the context of the overall Iraqi campaign concerning 'collateral damage', they found acceptable.

The viewer was well aware that restrictions on reporting were in operation during the Gulf War. This is not surprising given the findings of the content analysis: reporting restrictions or declarations of censored material were noted on 680 occasions, or 26 per cent of items. Table 28d shows, however, the origins of the censorship or reporting restrictions by country and the frequency across channels.

Table 28d. Origin of reporting restriction: channel comparisons

Originator	BBC1 N	BBC2 N	ITV N	C4 N	Sky N	CNN N	Total N	%
UK Government	14	4	–	1	4	–	23	3
UK Military	4	42	33	–	–	12	91	13
UK Other	5	2	2	–	–	3	15	2
US Government	–	–	2	5	1	1	9	1
US Military	8	2	4	1	12	70	97	14
US Other	5	2	2	1	1	3	14	2
Israeli Government	4	2	5	–	–	3	14	2
Israeli Military	1	14	1	–	–	36	52	8
Israeli Other	7	–	–	–	5	3	15	2
Saudi Government	1	1	–	–	1	9	12	2
Saudi Military	2	–	–	–	1	2	5	1
Saudi Other	5	1	–	–	3	1	10	2
Kuwait Military	–	–	–	–	–	–	–	–
Kuwait unspecified	–	–	–	–	–	–	–	–
Iraqi Government	59	19	42	4	12	44	180	26
Iraqi Military	–	–	–	–	–	–	–	–
Iraqi Other	17	9	3	3	13	9	54	8
Syrian Government	–	1	–	–	–	1	2	–
Syrian Military	1	–	–	–	–	–	1	–
Syrian unspecified	1	3	–	–	1	–	5	1
Other Government	–	–	–	–	–	–	–	–
Other Military	4	–	–	–	–	1	5	1
Other unspecified	30	9	1	–	1	–	41	6
Self censorship/restriction	16	–	7	–	1	3	27	4
Other censorship/restriction	–	2	–	–	–	6	8	1
Totals censored	184	113	102	15	56	207	680	99
Incidents of material	2209	1059	953	957	1257	1593	8028	
% of restricted footage	8	11	11	2	5	13	9	

One third (34 per cent) of all cases were imposed by Iraq. A further 18 per cent was imposed by the UK, and 17 per cent by the USA. Whereas government was attributed as the source of Iraqi restrictions, in the case of the UK and the USA, the majority of instances were attributed to military bodies – 81 per cent and 71 per cent of restrictions in the case of the UK and the USA respectively.

Those scenes which were restricted by the UK and the US military, were shots of military life, manoeuvres and equipment (36 per cent of UK military restrictions and 69 per cent of US). Restrictions imposed by Israeli government bodies was largely material showing damage to cities and towns (36 per cent of Israeli government restrictions). Israeli military bodies restricted material showing land attacks (24 per cent primarily Scud attacks), civilian life (16 per cent) and the damage caused to cities (20 per cent). Similarly the Iraqi government imposed restrictions on images of civilian life (18 per cent) and damage to cities (22 per cent).

The imposition of reporting restrictions by Israel in the above areas is easy to understand: Scud missiles are notoriously inaccurate when fired over long distances, and the Israelis did not wish to assist the Iraqis with target intelligence, by allowing television cameras to document where the missiles landed.

It is not quite so clear, however, why the Iraqis should impose reporting restrictions on damage to cities or civilian life, but no doubt similar reasons to that imposed by Israel were in operation. Nevertheless, such destruction, when seen in the West, would obviously have assisted Iraqi propaganda efforts and indeed, the lack of access given to coalition journalists to the claimed destruction that had taken place was counterproductive in that it cast doubt on whether much destruction had taken place. Viewers in the group discussions, for example, could not understand why, if widespread destruction had taken place as Iraqi spokesmen were claiming, they did not take coalition journalists to film and report on it. This lack of access to the claimed areas of destruction was, from the position of scoring propaganda points, doubly counterproductive since not only did it create suspicion in the minds of British viewers that no such destruction had occurred, but also allowed the coalition forces to advance claims for the effectiveness of 'smart weapons' that destroyed only military targets and installations. This failure by Iraq to exploit the propaganda war through restricting the movements of coalition journalists, probably resulted from Iraq not wishing to alarm its own citizens. But here we see the failure of Iraq at the most fundamental level, both as a military force and as a communicator. Not only was Iraq poor militarily when faced by the arranged might of advanced industrial nations, but poor in terms of waging a war of propaganda: to make unrealistic assertions to a civilian population about one's own military capacity creates demoralization when the promised and thus expected protection does not follow.

The content analysis can tell us nothing about how the war was explained to the population of Iraq, but all civilian populations do need such events explained and the acts of the participants made either legitimate or illegitimate. And part of that process is the explanation for the reasons for war. In so far then as the population of Britain was concerned, as we have already seen, very little historical analysis was provided by television to enable the viewer to situate and understand the war in terms of the wider unfolding of Middle Eastern politics. What television did do, however, was to give the immediate reasons for the hostilities, and lay out the objectives of the war. Even so, only one in eight (12 per cent) of items raised immediate reasons for the war. That is not too surprising since once battle is joined the story is really one of following events rather than tabling the reasons for the events. This procedure means, however, that in following war the news quickly settles into a presentation of acts rather than reasons for the action and thus takes attention away from fundamental issues such as the rationality of war, unless actors who wish to question the war can themselves manage to become a news event.

The most frequent reason given for hostilities by all channels was 'to liberate Kuwait', followed by 'to uphold international law' (Table 28e). Very few mentions were given to the part that the securing of an oil supply played as reason for the war. This is interesting in the light of the findings from the group discussions that viewers considered oil to be a major reason for the adoption of an armed response to Iraq's invasion of Kuwait. It would seem, therefore, that in the realm of understanding the rationale for political action the frequency of reasons given for a policy does not necessarily determine how the viewer will order the reasons in terms of primacy. What this means – and it is something worth considering in view of the attack of bias that is often made by politicians on television for over-representing or under-representing people or positions – is that the number of times a particular person or position is presented does not quantumly effect the attitudes of viewers when the position or reason that is represented runs counter to their understandings of the world. The viewers believed, and not just in the case of the Gulf, that political action is driven more by economic considerations than concern with justice.

76

Table 28e. Reasons for hostilities: channel comparisons

Reasons given for hostilities	BBC1 %	BBC2 %	ITV %	C4 %	Sky %	CNN %	Total %
To liberate Kuwait	31	57	91	84	58	44	54
To uphold international law	23	11	–	11	21	10	15
Fear of Hussein's expansion capacity	4	6	9	–	5	12	6
To ensure world-wide oil supply	4	3	–	5	–	10	4
Failure of diplomatic means	10	8	–	–	7	7	7
Other non-specified reason	29	15	0	0	8	17	14
Total %	101	100	100	100	99	100	100
Number of incidents	52	96	11	19	84	59	321
Total number of items	635	369	352	322	344	599	2621
% of items containing reasons	8	26	3	6	24	10	12

As well as showing the reasons given by the news for the war with Iraq, Table 28e also shows the reasons given on a channel-by-channel basis. As Table 28e shows, there are striking differences in the proportion of items that provided reasons for the war. ITV *News at Ten*, for example, gave reasons in only 3 per cent of items, whereas they occurred in one quarter of items on BBC2 *Newsnight* (26 per cent) and *Sky World News* (24 per cent). It would appear from Table 28e that BBC1, when compared to ITV, gave greater depth of coverage to the reasons for war than did ITV. ITV, for example, tended to give most of its account for reasons for war to the liberation of Kuwait, whilst BBC1 gave a greater range of reasons.

If we compare Table 28e – reasons for war – with Table 28f – objectives of war – what is interesting is that the news was more likely to feature the objectives of the war than reasons for the war. In other words, the news tended to adopt a political/militaristic perspective rather than a political/causation perspective. It must be pointed out, however, that discussion of the reasons for war often overlapped with discussion of the objectives of the hostilities. Nevertheless, these two aspects could be distinguished. A 'reason' was coded when a statement was made that provide the cause or motive for action, and 'objective' was coded when the intent or aim of military action was given. On this categorization the objectives of war appeared approximately twice as often as reasons given for war (24 per cent of items overall in contrast to 12 per cent of items stating reasons). What the news did, therefore, was to accept the military aims of the war – the removal of Iraqi forces from Kuwait and the destruction of Iraq's war machine – rather than feature the reasons for the war. BBC2, however, judging by Tables 28e and 28f, provided depth of coverage not just to the objectives of the war, but also to the reasons for war. CNN also covered both the objectives and reasons for war in depth by comparison with other channels – but they had more time to do it.

Table 28f. Objectives of war: channel comparisons

Objective of hostilities	BBC1 %	BBC2 %	ITV %	C4 %	Sky %	CNN %	Total %
To destroy Iraq's war machine	11	22	17	33	18	7	16
To remove Iraqi forces from Kuwait	61	40	57	41	56	54	52
To remove Hussein from power	13	24	17	15	9	24	18
To aid long-term stability in Middle East	4	12	10	8	10	6	8
Other non-specified objectives	12	2	–	3	7	9	6
Total %	101	100	101	100	100	100	100
Number of incidents	163	171	42	39	97	113	625
Total number of items	635	369	352	322	344	599	2621
% of items stating objectives	26	46	12	12	28	19	24

Politically, war is bound to be a difficult time for television companies. Faced with the massive challenge of covering a momentous event, often involving severe restrictions on reporting, the performance of television comes under greater scrutiny by politicians than perhaps on any other occasion. The content analysis therefore examined the appearance of politicians themselves on television. Table 29a shows the frequency of politicians interviewed by channel. (Politicians from all countries are included, not just those from the UK.) What is interesting about Table 29a, is that although the BBC is usually the channel that is singled out by the government of the day as not giving sufficient attention to government voice and over representing opposition voices – this was especially so during the Falkland Conflict – BBC1 was more likely, when compared to ITV, to interview politicians from government than those from opposition parties.

Table 29a. Frequency of politicians interviewed: channel comparisons

	BBC1 %	BBC2 %	ITV %	C4 %	Sky %	CNN %
Government	55	67	40	65	33	66
Opposition parties	45	33	60	35	66	33
Total %	100	100	100	100	99	99
Number of cases	110	66	50	159	54	9

However, it is one thing to note whether a politician represents the government or an opposition party, but a more important matter to note is what was said by those who appeared. The content analysis, therefore, categorizes speech into support for the war and criticism of the war.

On all channels the largest category of opinion given by politicians was one of total support for the war. However, as Table 29b shows, the proportion of politicians voicing criticism about the war, or Government handling of it, varied enormously between channels. *CNN News* did not include any criticism from politicians at all. On *Channel Four News*, ITV *News at Ten* and BBC1 *The Nine O'clock News*, criticism was rare at 9 per cent, 14 per cent and 14 per cent respectively. However, on *Sky World News* and BBC2 *Newsnight*, comparatively high proportions of comments made by political representatives were of a critical nature (24 per cent of reactions on *Sky World News* of which 17 per cent were criticisms of war in general and 7 per cent of government handling of it. On BBC2 *Newsnight* 21 per cent of reactions were critical of war in general, and a further 12 per cent were critical of the government handling of the war. The level of criticism on *Newsnight*, however, can largely be attributed to one programme where 10 Egyptian political representatives expressed their criticism of the war (22/1/91). The criticisms on *Sky World News*, on the other hand, were more evenly spread throughout the sample period. On the four of the six channels (ITV *News at Ten*, *Channel Four News*, *CNN News* and *Sky World News*) the majority of the criticism made not that of political attack on the policy of war, but concern over military aspects of the war.

Table 29b. Reaction by politicians: channel comparisons

	BBC1 %	BBC2 %	ITV %	C4 %	Sky %	CNN %
Total support	74	45	74	68	54	78
Qualified support	13	12	12	19	4	22
Neutral	–	9	–	3	18	–
Criticism of war (general)	10	21	10	6	17	–
Criticism of Government handling of war	4	12	4	3	7	–
Total %	101	99	100	99	100	100
Number of cases	110	66	50	159	54	9

What is perhaps surprising, given British television's fondness for opinion polls to judge the state of the parties or popularity of political leaders, was the absence of reference to public opinion on the war. Very few items, only 7 per cent, contained any reference to public opinion, of which only 2 per cent were substantiated with any statistical data. The warring of political parties would appear to warrant the judgement of the nation, but the warring of nations would not.

LEADERS

As well as analysing the appearance of politicians on television during the Gulf War, the content analysis also examined how the major leaders of the war were portrayed. Numerical analysis of news data indicated that the key figures worthy of detailed portrayal were: Saddam Hussein, George Bush, John Major, Perez de Cuellar and Mikhail Gorbachev.

One coding schedule was completed for each of the above leaders who was shown or mentioned more than once, or who spoke during a Gulf news item (more than one leader could be coded for any Gulf news item). In all 1078 schedules were completed; 60 per cent of these were for Saddam Hussein, 22 per cent George Bush, 10 per cent John Major, 5 per cent Mikhail Gorbachev and 3 per cent Perez de Cuellar.

The predominance given by television to Saddam Hussein may account for the fact that, in the sample of children surveyed, more knew the name of Saddam Hussein than they did that of George Bush or John Major. When asked 'Can you tell me the name of Iraq's military leader', 92 per cent named Saddam Hussein, compared to 80 per cent who correctly named the President of the United States, and 81 per cent who correctly named the Prime Minister of Great Britain. Knowledge of who was President of the United States, or who was the Prime Minister of Britain would not necessarily depend on the greater attention that children claimed they paid to television news during the Gulf War. Such knowledge is likely to have been a part of 'general knowledge'. Yet, nevertheless, it is interesting that Saddam Hussein was the most recognized leader and it is unlikely that his recognition is to be accounted for by reference to 'general knowledge'. It is highly likely, given the findings of the content analysis, that children recognized Saddam Hussein due to the absolute exposure he received on British television. The overall commander of the coalition forces was named correctly as Norman Schwartzkopf or 'Stormin' Norman' by only 37 per cent of children. Boys were much more likely to name him correctly than girls – 51 per cent and 19 per cent respectively; 30 per cent didn't know. This gender difference in knowledge gives support to the earlier argument about the heightened military interest that the boys showed in the war.

It is not just the sheer exposure of Saddam Hussein that is interesting in the way television presented events in the Gulf, but also the manner of his portrayal. Indeed, television's handling of the various leaders tended to personalize the war around the figure of Saddam, in a way that was not the case with other leaders. But before examining this aspect of coverage let us look at levels and forms of exposure.

Although Perez de Cuellar appeared in a relatively small number of items, one third of these were leading story-lines and featured in the first item on the news bulletin, for example: 'UN Secretary General Perez de Cuellar returns home with no deal' (Sky, 14/10/91). In contrast only 14 per cent of either Saddam Hussein's or John Major's coverage formed lead stories, compared with one-fifth of both George Bush's (22 per cent) and Mikhail Gorbachev's (23 per cent) coverage.

Table 30a shows the proportion of incidents where leaders were seen talking, and those which included references to them, discussions of them or footage where the leader was not talking.

Over three-quarters of incidents that showed John Major (80 per cent) and Perez de Cuellar (77 per cent) and two-thirds (64 per cent) of George Bush showed them talking to camera. In contrast in only one-third (35 per cent) of the instances that showed Mikhail Gorbachev and less than one-fifth (18 per cent) for Saddam Hussein were the leaders shown talking on screen and thus involved attributed rather than observed features.

Given the differential access to the various leaders, the findings of Table 30a are not surprising, but they do mean that the role of attribution in the case of Gorbachev, and in particular, Saddam, have great importance. Table 30b shows the qualities attributed to the leaders.

The 'devious deeds' category used in Table 30b was a category designed to record a host of negative comments and accusations made against a leader's character. This could include references to manipulation, untrustworthiness, untruthfulness, and so on. Saddam Hussein was highly scored in this category. Indeed, as Table 30b shows, Saddam Hussein was the clear leader when it came to negative estimation of his character. For example, where a quality was attributed to Saddam Hussein, 90 per cent fell into a negative category – 'The allied prisoners in President Saddam's vindictive hands' (ITV, 21/01/91). One-quarter were coded as devious deed; for example, placing civilians in military bunkers, firing on Israel to try to bring it into the war.

81

Table 30a. Frequency of incidents where leader was shown talking

	Shown talking %	Reference to discussions of %	Total %	Number of incidents %
Saddam Hussein	18	82	100	646
George Bush	64	36	100	236
John Major	80	20	100	108
Mikhail Gorbachev	35	65	100	51
Perez de Cuellar	77	23	100	31

Table 30b. Qualities attributed to leaders

Quality attributed	Hussein %	Bush %	Major %	De Cuellar %	Gorbachev %
Positive leadership qualities	5	45	74	–	75
Negative leadership qualities	19	15	5	67	25
Positive military qualities	3	11	–	–	–
Negative military qualities	15	3	–	–	–
Positive mental ability	–	7	–	–	–
Negative mental ability	5	–	–	–	–
Positive humanitarianism	1	7	16	33	–
Negative humanitarianism	27	3	–	–	–
Suggestion of devious deeds	23	7	5	–	–
Total %	98	98	100	100	100
Number of incidents	489	74	19	3	4

Note that due to rounding of percentages in summary tables, percentages may be given as 100 per cent ±2 per cent.

It is not surprising, given this 'bad press', that the viewers in the group discussions considered Saddam as 'evil'. In contrast to Saddam Hussein, 70 per cent of the qualities attributed to George Bush were positive. Over one-half were comments on his positive leadership qualities – no doubt a reflection on the fact that it was America and Bush that were actually driving the coalition team. Frequencies for John Major, Perez de Cuellar and Mikhail Gorbachev are relatively low, but it is worth noting in Table 30b the higher incidence of positive qualities attributed to John Major (90 per cent) and Mikhail Gorbachev (75 per cent) in contrast to the higher negative leadership qualities of Perez de Cuellar (67 per cent).

Where statements were actually made by the leaders themselves, these were most likely to be expressions of government (31 per cent) or personal opinion (34 per cent), rather than the opinion of the nation (4 per cent) or reference to religious belief (2 per cent). Nevertheless, differences between leaders are evident. Saddam Hussein and Perez de Cuellar were more frequently seen expressing their personal opinions than government ones whilst the reverse is true for George Bush, John Major and Mikhail Gorbachev.

The offering of personal opinion by Saddam Hussein, rather than speaking on the behalf of some wider authority, such as the state or the people, undoubtedly helped to personalize the war and focus attention on Saddam as an individual historical actor rather than part of an alignment of political forces. This type of focus on Saddam Hussein more than likely aided the development of the view which the viewers held of him as unreasonable – the idea of unreasonableness or madness is usually restricted to an individual and not a state. Thus focusing on Saddam Hussein, biographically free-floating from political aspirations of party, state or nation, favoured the coalition side's presentation of itself as the exasperated face of reason, and Iraq's face as one of unreason. Of course, the attitudes that were found in the group discussions towards Saddam Hussein/Iraq, were not formed purely, or even mainly, from the manner in which television focused on the Iraqi leader. The viewers were well aware that the coalition forces drew their moral right from the collected decision of the nations making up the United Nations. The portrayal of Saddam Hussein, and the manner in which he was portrayed, served to reinforce viewers' judgements that had been formed in the course of following the United Nations proceedings.

Although Saddam Hussein personalized the war by the presentation of his own opinion rather than showing himself as acting as a spokesman for a nation, television nevertheless assisted this process by linking him directly with acts and materials in a way that did not occur with respect to coalition leaders. For example, a total of 213 military acts were attributed directly to leaders, but in nearly all instances (93 per cent) these were attributed to Saddam Hussein, of which the majority were the bombing of civilians (26 per cent) and the mistreatment of troops (22 per cent) – 'He parades captive allied airman' (BBC1, 20/01/91). Furthermore, although few items attributed ownership of armies or weaponry directly to leaders, in all cases where this did happen (10 per cent armies, 7 per cent weaponry) this was attributed to Saddam Hussein – e.g. 'Saddam Hussein in Kuwait takes personal control of his forces' (BBC1 16/01/91). Table 30c shows the channel differences in relation to the attribution of armed forces to Saddam Hussein.

Table 30c. Attribution of armed forces to Saddam Hussein: channel comparisons

Attribution	BBC1 %	BBC2 %	ITV %	C4 %	Sky %	CNN %
National army	26	1	–	10	10	7
Saddam Hussein's army	3	14	28	8	33	39
Both	27	–	1	–	1	5
No mention	44	84	71	83	46	49
Total %	100	99	100	101	101	100
Number of cases	186	147	78	52	92	87

On all channels, except BBC 1 (*The Nine O'Clock News*) and C4 (*Channel 4 News*), the opposing force were most frequently referred to as Saddam Hussein's rather than Iraqi forces. Ownership of weaponry on BBC1 (*The Nine O'Clock News*) and C4 (*Channel 4 News*) was more frequently referred to as Iraq's (19 per cent) rather than Saddam Hussein's (5 per cent). *CNN News* showed the highest proportional frequency for the attribution of weaponry directly to Saddam Hussein at 34 per cent; *Sky World News* 20 per cent; ITV (*News at Ten*) 18 per cent; BBC2 (*Newsnight*) 1 per cent. C4 (*Channel 4 News*) had no cases.

This attribution of armies and weaponry on the one hand to a state, and on the other to a person, reflects the two distinct traditions of the press – the quality press tradition and the popular press tradition. The personalizing of politics, championed by Lord Northcliffe with the founding of the *Daily Mail* in 1896, is the hallmark of the popular press. On the evidence of Table 30c, ITV and CNN clearly fall into the camp of the popular press tradition, and BBC1 and *Channel Four News* into the quality press tradition. (The personalization exhibited by BBC2 is probably a result of *Newsnight*'s more current affairs interview format.)

What the actual affect on the viewer is of attaching armies or weaponry to a leader rather than a nation is an intriguing question. Winston Churchill, however, was in little doubt, and wrote a memo to the Ministry of Information during the Second World War to the effect that given the obvious enthusiasm of the German people for the laying waste of Europe, perhaps it would be appropriate to inform the British people that the war was against Germany and not just Hitler – most of the newsreels up until the Casablanca Conference of 1942 and the formulation of the policy of Unconditional Surrender, had tended to present the conflict in terms of Hitler's war.

What form propaganda takes depends, to a large extent, not just on the aims of war, but also the aims of peace. The move, therefore, to Unconditional Surrender of Germany in the Second World War with the aim of total subjugation, meant the necessity of including the German people as accountable and not just their leaders. The reverse was the case in the First World War. Initially the Great War had been had been cast as the rise of Prussian Militarism, to change towards the end of the conflict to become the Kaiser's War as propaganda efforts were aimed at focusing the conflict on the leaders with the offer to the German people that once its leaders were removed, then as a nation it could return to rejoin the rest of the peaceable European community. In short, it did not suit the peace aims of Britain to include the German people as responsible for the First World War, but it did in the Second World War.

In terms of the War in the Gulf the official coalition propaganda line was that the war was restricted to the removal of the Iraqi forces from Kuwait, and not to the overthrow of Saddam Hussein. There was, however, suspicion in various quarters that the hidden agenda did include the overthrow of Saddam – and various coalition spokesmen indicated that they would not be sorry if Saddam's removal was a consequence of military actions – but at no time did coalition spokesmen explicitly state that this was their real purpose.

ITV *News at Ten* and *CNN News*, in following the popular press tradition of personalizing politics and attributing armed forces and weaponry to Saddam Hussein, thus tended to provide an account of events that more easily led to the creation of an image of responsibility in tune with the hidden propaganda agenda than that of BBC1 *Nine O'Clock News* and *Channel Four News*. BBC1 *Nine O'Clock News* and *Channel Four News*, on the other hand, by their adoption of the quality press tradition of refusing to personalize politics, tended to provide an account of events where the image of accountability was closer to the official propaganda of the coalition forces.

There is no suggestion here that any of the various channels' news presentations followed one particular propaganda agenda or another. The attempt of this analysis is to show, drawing on the content analysis, that different news traditions can facilitate different propaganda purposes. And that the style of the BBC, with its quality press tradition of referring to the opposing forces by the name of the state from which they were drawn rather than by the name of its leader was, in functional terms, more in keeping with the coalition's official propaganda than that of ITV

85

and CNN which, operating within the popular press tradition, personalized the news and referred to the Iraqi forces as 'Saddam's army'.

Propaganda goals move, as we have seen in the case of the First and Second World War as government aims for mobilizing opinion move to accommodate their ambitions for war and for peace. It is useful analytically, therefore, to examine the various television channels' news traditions and understand the opportunity they provide for the support of the intentional propaganda of government, rather than seek for signs that particular channels favour a particular political stance. At the very least such a framework of understanding allows the presentation of images to be set within the dynamic flow of political movement and change.

The viewers in the group discussions demonstrated confusion as to how far to include the Iraqi people in their wrath at the invasion of Kuwait, or whether to restrict their anger solely to their leader. Whilst not entirely absolving Iraq as a people, the overwhelming position adopted was to lay the blame for the death and destruction of the war at Saddam's feet. This is not surprising. Where a leader is seen to be the embodiment of a nation it is highly likely that a war will be seen not just to be conducted in his or her name, but that acts within the war will, by extension, be seen as directed by the leader rather than a product of wider forces. But the point is, on a channel-by-channel basis, ITV *News at Ten* and *CNN News* fed into a view of events that not only placed Saddam Hussein in the centre stage of history more than BBC1 *Nine O'Clock News* and *Channel Four News* did, but in doing so fostered the culpability of Saddam Hussein to a greater extent than BBC1 *Nine O'Clock News* or *Channel Four News*. But before commenting on the possible ramifications of personalizing the war we ought to turn directly to the accountability of leaders for events in the war as provided by television and away from accountability through personalization of forces and weaponry.

When it came to the portrayal of Saddam Hussein, television news was judgemental. In almost one-half (48 per cent) of occasions when Saddam Hussein was referred to he was either praised or blamed for events in the war. In contrast judgemental comment on other leaders was rarely made – 13 per cent of occasions for George Bush, 6 per cent for John Major, and no cases for Mikhail Gorbachev and Perez de Cuellar. Where praise or blame was apportioned, Saddam Hussein was most frequently blamed for events – 91 per cent of occasions for blame – whereas John Major was most frequently praised – 50 per cent, with George Bush 40 per cent.

To determine the extent to which the coverage of the Gulf War focused on Saddam Hussein as the enemy rather than Iraqi forces, then for each item which included references to, discussions of, or actually showed Saddam Hussein talking, details of his actions and characteristics attributed to him were noted.

Nearly one-quarter (24 per cent) of items which included Saddam Hussein inferred or stated that he had the ability to end the war by withdrawing from Kuwait – 'The smoking gun. New appeals to Saddam, but he is defiant' (Sky, 16/01/91).

One-quarter of items (23 per cent) also speculated how he could be removed from Kuwait. The majority (28 per cent) of these favoured a rebellion within Iraq. Only 7 per cent suggested the use of external force or taking him prisoner (5 per cent and 2 per cent respectively).

One-fifth (20 per cent) of items made reference to Saddam Hussein's possibility of governing Iraq after the cessation of hostilities. Of these only 15 per cent suggested that he would remain as leader, whilst 85 per cent speculated that he would lose his premiership.

This heavy speculation by television that Saddam Hussein would not be able to maintain his leadership position after the war is worth considering in terms of its possible consequences for how the British public viewed the success of the war. Such speculation may well have created for the viewer the idea that the removal of Saddam Hussein was not only a war aim, but that success in the war was to be largely determined by his removal – the hidden war aim – and not just the removal of the Iraqi army from Kuwait.

It would be interesting to survey now the viewers' judgement of the war and see if attitudes towards it have changed in the light of Saddam's ability to survive military defeat. Given the unfavourable and vitriolic comments made in the group discussions towards Saddam Hussein, and on the evidence of the content analysis showing the negative image that television presented of Saddam Hussein, it is likely that disappointment, if not anger, exists on the part of the public to the fact that such a man has managed, or been allowed, to retain power.

Messages that are functional for government in one situation can be carried over to become dysfunctional in other situations, and it might well be that any call for support for military action, be it in Iraq or elsewhere, will not be so readily forthcoming if the public believes that such action is inconclusive. It was obvious in the group discussions, for example, that sanctions were not preferred to military action as a way of forcing Iraq out of Kuwait, not because military action was a preferred way of conducting international politics, but because they were held to have been ineffective in the case of South Africa. In short, it helps in gaining public support for a policy, if it is believed that the policy will be effective. But, and this is what is intriguing when the results of the content analysis are laid over political policy – it was not at all clear what the political policy, apart from the immediate aim of removing the Iraqi forces from Kuwait, was in the Gulf. And certainly, whilst the removal of Saddam Hussein was never a stated aim of the coalition, the viewers talked with in the group discussions had difficulty countenancing an outcome that entailed Saddam Hussein remaining in power. The removal of Saddam Hussein, for the viewers talked with, looked as if it was an aim of the war. And that impression, or perhaps more accurately, feeling, came from watching the news and how Saddam Hussein was talked about and presented.

IMAGES OF DEATH AND INJURY

In both the survey and the group discussions, attention was paid to the acceptability by the viewer of images of death and injury appearing in the news. The content analysis, therefore, examined the amount and nature of scenes of death and injury that appeared during the War.

The military offensives reported in the news were mainly air attacks. These formed one-third (33 per cent) of such coverage. Land attacks formed one-fifth (19 per cent), and land missile attacks 15 per cent. Sea attacks featured infrequently at 4 per cent whilst combinations of these types of attacks formed 28 per cent. When coverage of these offensives included scenes where injuries and/or deaths to people occurred a violence aspect schedule was completed to determine the extent and nature of the portrayal of injury or death.

Although the popular imagery of war may revolve around killing, in the case of the Gulf War only 105 schedules were completed for items containing scenes which portrayed the results of military action in terms of human casualties. These scenes added up to three and a half hours – 210 minutes of television time representing only 3 per cent of the total Gulf output, and amounted to 7 per cent of the total time spent on Military Aspects.

One-half (51 per cent) of all these occurrences were located in Iraq, followed by one-quarter (24 per cent) in Israel, 10 per cent in Saudi Arabia and 9 per cent in Kuwait. Coalition forces (including UK and US forces) were seen to initiate violence in 61 per cent of cases, whilst Iraq contributed 38 per cent. The initiator of violence was defined as the country responsible for inflicting injury or death. If, therefore, the initiator of violence was most usually the coalition forces, Iraq was most usually the victim – 57 per cent of cases, followed by Israel 24 per cent, Saudi Arabia 4 per cent, Kuwait 3 per cent and Jordan 2 per cent. The coalition side were seen as victims of violence in only 10 per cent of cases. (Table 31a shows the declared source of attack which caused injury to people.)

Well over half (60 per cent) of items depicting injury were shown in conjunction with pictures of military action. Of these 87 per cent showed bombing, 5 per cent explosives, 3 per cent shooting and 2 per cent the use of chemical weapons featured in archive footage.

The frequency for the types of injury caused by military action are given in Table 31b. It must be noted that several different types of injury may be seen in any one item.

Table 31a. Source of injury to people

Source	Number	%
Ground troops	7	7
Terrorist	–	–
Plane, tank, ship	56	53
Land launched missile	31	30
Mine	3	3
Other	8	8
Totals	105	101

Table 31b. Types of injuries caused

Type of injury	Number	%
Dazed, confused	24	15
Minor injuries	33	21
Burns	21	13
Broken limbs	31	20
Dying people	6	4
Dead bodies (covered)	23	15
Dead bodies (uncovered)	12	8
Other	7	5
Total	157	101

Table 31c. Distribution of injured people

Country	Troops		Males		Civilian females		Children		Total injured	
	N	%	N	%	N	%	N	%	N	%
Allies	26	58	–	–	–	–	–	–	26	13
Iraq	7	16	34	57	11	38	61	97	113	57
Israel	–	–	24	40	18	62	2	3	44	22
Kuwait	–	–	1	2	–	–	–	–	1	1
Jordan	–	–	1	2	–	–	–	–	1	1
Saudi Arabia	12	27	–	–	–	–	–	–	12	6
Total	45	101	60	101	29	100	63	100	197	100

Table 31d. Distribution of dead people

Country	Number of troops	Number of civilians			Total dead
		Males	Females	Children	
Iraq	105	104	38	36	283
Israel	–	9	–	–	9
Kuwait	–	1	–	–	1
Jordan	–	3	–	–	3
Saudi Arabia	–	1	–	–	1
Total	105	118	38	36	297

Of all the injuries shown, one-fifth (21 per cent) covered minor injuries, one-third (33 per cent) showed serious injuries (burns and broken limbs), while just over one-quarter (27 per cent) showed dead or dying people.

Tables 31c and 31d show the frequency of injured and dead people by their status – that is, whether they were troops or civilians – and their ethnicity. Three-quarters (75 per cent) of injury shown were depictions of injury to civilian personnel.

Considering that the sample period covered a range of attacks and full scale battles, the number of people shown to be injured is remarkably low at only 197. Children, however, were seen injured more frequently than any other group, providing nearly one-third (31 per cent) of all casualties. These were predominantly Iraqi children, and is interesting when set within the context of the 'battle for hearts and minds' that war involves.

We have already seen, in the audience section of the findings, that a large majority of the population – two-thirds – considered that it was a 'good thing' to have British and American journalists report from Baghdad. One-third (29 per cent) however disagreed, and would have preferred journalists from the coalition side not to have been in Baghdad on the grounds that they could only 'report what the Iraqis wanted them to' (see Table 6). The finding in the content analysis that the pictures of injury to civilian populations shown on British screens consisted mainly of Iraqi children lends some support to such fears.

Although propaganda has many elements to it, that part which has attempted to appeal to the sentiments and feelings of people for the suffering of others has generally featured children. Indeed, throughout the history of war propaganda the suffering and torment of children has formed a key part – the innocence that attaches to children allows the presentation of the opposition as the unjust brutal aggressor. The fact, therefore, that most of the injured Iraqis that were shown on British television came from the ranks of children helps show the directed nature of the news coming out of Baghdad. That is, although there can be no doubt that Iraqi children were injured and killed as a result of the coalition strikes, Iraqi officials clearly saw it in their interest to direct coalition journalists to sources where injured children would be found in order to highlight that aspect or consequence of the war above other aspects and consequences. It ought to be remembered, however, that despite this 'direction' – and most viewers were aware as the surveyed results show that the reports from Iraq were compiled under Iraqi control – the majority of people still considered it to be worthwhile having British and American journalists report from Baghdad.

Military personnel contributed to nearly one-quarter (23 per cent) of injured people seen. Of these, the majority (58 per cent) were from the coalition forces, followed by 27 per cent Saudi Arabian troops. Only 15 per cent of the injured that were seen were Iraqi military personnel. Civilian males were seen twice as often as civilian females (60 injured civilian males, 29 injured civilian females). Whilst the majority of injured males were Iraqi (57 per cent of injured males) the majority of injured females were Israeli (62 per cent of injured females).

The number of dead bodies shown in items depicting violence was somewhat higher than the number of injured people shown. One-third (33 per cent) of items depicted dead bodies. In these scenes over 600 dead bodies were counted. (This figure is increased due to the inclusion of one scene shown on BBC1 (*The Nine O'Clock News*) which included

91

brief footage of an Iraqi morgue where there were too many bodies to count reliably – but estimated at approximately 300. Thus, if this scene is excluded from the data, the number of dead bodies which could be coded was reduced to 297). The distribution of the dead in terms of status and ethnicity is given in Table 31d.

Nearly all (95 per cent) of the dead people shown were Iraqis. Dead Iraqi civilians far outnumbered dead Iraqi troops – 62 per cent of Iraqi dead were civilians, compared to 37 per cent who were Iraqi troops.

The dead from countries other than Iraq, particularly Kuwait, Israel and Saudi Arabia featured infrequently. The location of the violent scenes was mostly at the site of an attack in an urban area (59 per cent). Hospitalized victims were shown in 29 per cent of cases.

Few items showed disturbed or traumatized victims. Hysteria was noted in 15 per cent of cases, whilst no emotional response, or a very muted one, was recorded in 57 per cent of cases. The graphic content of items showing injury or death was also muted. One-third (31 per cent) of these items showed no blood at all, and a further 57 per cent showed 'only some blood'. Scenes with a lot of blood were noted in only 11 per cent of cases. However, while only one-half (50 per cent) of scenes were judged to be mild in graphic detail, nearly four in ten (38 per cent) were considered to be disturbing, and 12 per cent were coded as horrific. A dramatic example of a horrific report was a sequence shown on Sky (1/02/91) after the taking of Khafji where the camera followed a trail of blood to the sound of running feet.

REACTION

It is unclear how many people lost their lives in the war, but the estimate is generally put at somewhere around 100,000 Iraqi troops, 5000 civilians and less than 500 coalition forces. What is clear, therefore, is that very little of the death and injury that occurred in the war was actually seen on television. But this is not to say that the British viewer was denied knowledge of the extent of the killing that took place – it was reported, but simply not seen. However, where cameras were present, mainly in civilian settings of the war zone, pictures were taken. But even there, the amount of graphic detail shown would appear, judging from the content analysis, to have been limited. Again, however, it is not as if the British viewer was unaware of the terrible injuries that had been inflicted on the Iraqis: some close-up shots of the dead and injured were shown. Also, the news did on occasion mention terrible injury had occurred, but gave justification for not showing the pictures of the injured and dead.

Michael Buerk (BBC1 13/02/91):

> You should be aware that many of the pictures from Baghdad of the burnt bodies of the victims were considered too grim to show.

Julia Somerville (ITV 13/02/91):

> The Iraqis didn't censor any part of Brent Sadler's report, but we at ITN did edit out some scenes because we regarded them as too distressing to broadcast.

The debate about how much detail of death and injury to show in war will continue – fuelled, in part, by the belief, especially after the Vietnam War, that the close televised coverage of armed conflict can stop war.

Wars are ended by defeat and begun with the sure certainty that much horror will follow. Indeed, regardless of whether war is at close quarters or removed, the knowledge and portrayal of it make little difference to its course and whose causes rest outside the shock of events as they unfold. Political and power arrangements make war more or less likely, not sentimentality. Of course, the public's or viewers' response cannot be ignored by government, and the 'lessons' of Vietnam stay to haunt democratic administrations. But if there is a media lesson to be drawn from Vietnam, it is not the effect of pictures on American morale, but the shattering effects of information on an unprepared public because it was uninformed about the course and nature of the struggle in South East Asia. All governments must have their citizens accept the cost of death and injury that inevitably follows from war as a legitimate price for a correct political policy. And that is precisely what the American television networks could not deliver to their audience with Vietnam – death with sense.

We have seen from the responses to the survey, and from the detailed conversations recorded in the group discussions, that the British viewer did accept the war in the Gulf as correct and just. The tolerance to accepting death and injury, because the cause was seen as just, is therefore likely to have been very high. However, as we have seen from the content analysis of the main news programmes, that tolerance was never really tested – very few pictures of death and injury were broadcast. We have no knowledge, therefore, of what the response might have been had the viewer seen the full carnage on the road to Basra inflicted on the Iraqi troops as they fled Kuwait at the end of the war. Would they have supported continued aggression and more death, even of the enemy, as the price of removing Saddam Hussein as the president of Iraq? We do not know. But we do know, from the survey and the group discussions, that the British viewer does not wish to be exposed to the visual horrors of war. Although they might complain at gaps in picture coverage of events, they do not appear to want to be visually dragged into the charnel house of events themselves. Whether television should do so, is a political and moral question.

Appendix 1

Adult survey

Interviews were conducted in-home, and lasted on average 55 minutes. The survey was based upon an initial random location sample of 88 sampling points (GB Census Enumeration Districts). Within each sampling point, quotas were set for age, sex and social grade (all interlocked) so as to ensure that the population was represented accurately. Quotas were set from BARB Establishment data. In all, 981 adults aged 16+ were interviewed in Great Britain. Further interviews were conducted in Northern Ireland. Further controls were set for working status within sex. All interviews were conducted by Research International professional interviewers, trained to IQCS standards. All interviews were conducted between 13 and 25 March 1991.

A further boost sample of 100 individuals living in broadband cable homes were interviewed, so as to ensure that sufficient viewers of the CNN news channel were interviewed. Quotas for these were set according to BARB data.

All data shown in the study are based on weighted data. Weights were applied to the merged GB and Northern Ireland samples to ensure that the total main sample was representative of the UK in terms of age, sex and social grade distributions reported by BARB's 1990 Establishment survey. Details of the weighted and unweighted samples are shown below. Unless otherwise stated, all percentages shown are based upon the total sample. In some cases, total percentages may not sum up to 100 per cent due to rounding.

The field work was carried out by the market research company, Research International.

Appendix 2

Children's and group discussions survey

A sample of 212 children aged between 9 and 15 were interviewed by survey. These were drawn from the households in which the main sample of adults were interviewed. The children were selected from all the EDs sampled, with quotas set for age and sex. The interviews were conducted in-home and lasted between 10 and 15 minutes. The field work was carried out by the market research company, Research International.

Group discussions

A series of 4 group discussions with children was held, structured as follows:

Group 1:   Girls, aged 10–12 years old, BC1C2, North

Group 2:   Boys, aged 13–15 years old, BC1C2, North

Group 3:   Boys, aged 10–12 years old, BC1C2, South

Group 4:   Girls, aged 13–15 years old, BC1C2, North

The permission of the children's parents was secured prior to the discussion, and sensitive ethnic or religious groups were screened out, as were those children who had friends or family serving in the Gulf at the time of the research.

The groups were conducted in Staines, Middlesex, and Ilkley, West Yorkshire, on 27 and 26 February 1991 respectively.

Groups 3 and 4 were conducted immediately prior to the land war, which had commenced by the time Groups 1 and 2 were held.

The groups were moderated by Dr Alison Lyon, of the market research company Counterpoint, which specializes in research with children, and Dr David Morrison of the University of Leeds.

Appendix 3

Adult group discussions

The results of the group discussions are based on ten group discussions carried out in mid-March of 1991, consisting of eight to ten respondents per group. The groups were each single sex – five male and five female – and were further split by age and social grade as set out below.

1	Male	C1/C2	16–34
2	Female	C1/C2	16–34
3	Male	C1/C2	35–34
4	Female	C1/C2	35–55
5	Male	C1/C2	16–34
6	Female	C1/C2	35–55
7	Male	AB	16–34
8	Female	AB	16–34
9	Male	AB	35–55
10	Female	AB	35–55

The groups were carried out in three geographical areas of the country – The North (Leeds), the Midlands (Birmingham), the South (London).

The respondents were required to be very or fairly interested in news/current affairs programmes. Students were excluded from the groups, as were those connected in any way with the armed forces.

One further criterion placed on each group was that it should be evenly divided between those who normally preferred BBC as a channel and those who normally preferred ITV.

It was originally intended to conduct only six discussion groups consisting of C1/C2 viewers. However, following the completion of a few group discussions and discovering the high level of support for the war, it was decided to extend the number of groups to include AB viewers in case the educated 'liberal' anti-war viewer was being overlooked due to class bias.

As an aid to understanding how viewers actually interpret and understand the news, all participants to the groups were shown four pieces of film of the attack on the Amiriya bunker/shelter in the suburb of Baghdad on 13 February 1991. These bulletins were from BBC1, ITN and TF1, the French channel. Also shown was some raw footage of the bunker/shelter attacks shot by the news agency, WTN, but not shown uncut by ITN on the grounds that it contained scenes which were considered too harrowing for viewers.

The Groups were moderated by Dr David Morrison, University of Leeds.

Media titles available from John Libbey

ACAMEDIA RESEARCH MONOGRAPHS

Satellite Television in Western Europe
Richard Collins
Hardback ISBN 0 86196 203 6

Beyond the Berne Convention
Copyright, Broadcasting and the Single European Market
Vincent Porter
Hardback ISBN 0 86196 267 2

The Media Dilemma:
Freedom and Choice or Concentrated Power?
Gareth Locksley
Hardback ISBN 0 86196 230 3

Nuclear Reactions: A Study in Public Issue Television
John Corner, Kay Richardson and Natalie Fenton
Hardback ISBN 0 86196 251 6

Transnationalization of Television in Western Europe
Preben Sepstrup
Hardback ISBN 0 86196 280 X

The People's Voice: Local Television and Radio in Europe
Nick Jankowski, Ole Prehn and James Stappers
Hardback ISBN 0 86196 322 9

BBC ANNUAL REVIEWS

Annual Review of BBC Broadcasting Research: No XV - 1989
Peter Menneer (ed)
Paperback ISBN 0 86196 209 5

Annual Review of BBC Broadcasting Research: No XVI - 1990
Peter Menneer (ed)
Paperback ISBN 0 86196 265 6

Annual Review of BBC Broadcasting Research: No XVII - 1991
Peter Menneer (ed)
Paperback ISBN 0 86196 319 9

Media titles available from John Libbey

BROADCASTING STANDARDS COUNCIL PUBLICATIONS

A Measure of Uncertainty: The Effects of the Mass Media
Guy Cumberbatch and Dennis Howitt
Hardback ISBN 0 86196 231 1

Violence in Television Fiction: Public Opinion and Broadcasting Standards
David Docherty
Paperback ISBN 0 86196 284 2

Survivors and the Media
Ann Shearer
Paperback ISBN 0 86196 332 6

Taste and Decency in Broadcasting
Andrea Millwood Hargrave
Paperback ISBN 0 86196 331 8

A Matter of Manners? – The Limits of Broadcast Language
Edited by Andrea Millwood Hargrave
Paperback ISBN 0 86196 337 7

BROADCASTING RESEARCH UNIT MONOGRAPHS

**Quality in Television –
Programmes, Programme-makers, Systems**
Richard Hoggart (ed)
Paperback ISBN 0 86196 237 0

Keeping Faith? Channel Four and its Audience
David Docherty, David E. Morrison and Michael Tracey
Paperback ISBN 0 86196 158 7

**Invisible Citizens:
British Public Opinion and the Future of Broadcasting**
David E. Morrison
Paperback ISBN 0 86196 111 0

School Television in Use
Diana Moses and Paul Croll
Paperback ISBN 0 86196 308 3

Media titles available from John Libbey

UNIVERSITY OF MANCHESTER BROADCASTING SYMPOSIUM

And Now for the BBC ...
Proceedings of the 22nd Symposium 1991
Nod Miller and Rod Allen (eds)
Paperback ISBN 0 86196 318 0

Published in association with UNESCO

Video World-Wide: An International Study
Manuel Alvarado (ed)
Paperback ISBN 0 86196 143 9

Published in association with THE ARTS COUNCIL of GREAT BRITAIN

Picture This: Media Representations of Visual Art and Artists
Philip Hayward (ed)
Paperback ISBN 0 86196 126 9

Culture, Technology and Creativity
Philip Hayward (ed)
Paperback ISBN 0 86196 266 4

ITC TELEVISION RESEARCH MONOGRAPHS

Television in Schools
Robin Moss, Christopher Jones and Barrie Gunter
Hardback ISBN 0 86196 314 8

Media titles available from John Libbey

IBA TELEVISION RESEARCH MONOGRAPHS

Teachers and Television:
A History of the IBA's Educational Fellowship Scheme
Josephine Langham
Hardback ISBN 0 86196 264 8

Godwatching: Viewers, Religion and Television
Michael Svennevig, Ian Haldane, Sharon Spiers and Barrie Gunter
Hardback ISBN 0 86196 198 6 Paperback ISBN 0 86196 199 4

Violence on Television: What the Viewers Think
Barrie Gunter and Mallory Wober
Hardback ISBN 0 86196 171 4 Paperback ISBN 0 86196 172 2

Home Video and the Changing Nature of Television Audience
Mark Levy and Barrie Gunter
Hardback ISBN 0 86196 175 7 Paperback ISBN 0 86196 188 9

Patterns of Teletext Use in the UK
Bradley S. Greenberg and Carolyn A. Lin
Hardback ISBN 0 86196 174 9 Paperback ISBN 0 86196 187 0

Attitudes to Broadcasting Over the Years
Barrie Gunter and Michael Svennevig
Hardback ISBN 0 86196 173 0 Paperback ISBN 0 86196 184 6

Television and Sex Role Stereotyping
Barrie Gunter
Hardback ISBN 0 86196 095 5 Paperback ISBN 0 86196 098 X

Television and the Fear of Crime
Barrie Gunter
Hardback ISBN 0 86196 118 8 Paperback ISBN 0 86196 119 6

Behind and in Front of the Screen - Television's Involvement with Family Life
Barrie Gunter and Michael Svennevig
Hardback ISBN 0 86196 123 4 Paperback ISBN 0 86196 124 2